THE VIJAYANAGAR EMPIRE

CHRONICLES OF PAES AND NUNIZ

THE VIJAYANAGAR EMPIRE
CHRONICLES OF PAES AND NUNIZ

NARRATIVE OF DOMINGOS PAES
(WRITTEN, PROBABLY A. D. 1520-22)

OF THE THINGS WHICH I SAW AND CONTRIVED TO LEARN CONCERNING THE KINGDOM OF NARSIMGA ETC.

CHRONICLE OF FERNAO NUNIZ
(WRITTEN PROBABLY, A.D. 1535-37)

GYAN

Published by

GYAN

Gyan Publishing House
5, Ansari Road
Daryaganj, New Delhi-110002
Phone: 011-47034999, 9811692060
E-mail: books@gyanbooks.com

Distribution Network
gyanbooks.com
India, USA, Canada, UK, Australia, France

ISBN : 978-81-212-4185-4 (PB)
First Published, London, 1900

2nd Impression 2020

Printed at: Gyan Press, Delhi.

The Vijayanagar Empire Chronicles of Paes and Nuniz
Author: Chronicle of Fernao Nuniz

CHRONICLES OF PAES AND NUNIZ

LETTER

(? TO THE HISTORIAN BARROS) WHICH ACCOMPANIED THE CHRONICLES WHEN SENT FROM INDIA TO PORTUGAL ABOUT THE YEAR 1537 A.D.

SINCE I have lived till now in this city (? Goa), it seemed necessary to do what your Honour desired of me, namely, to search for men who had formerly been in Bisnaga; for I know that no one goes there without bringing away his quire of paper written about its affairs. Thus I obtained this summary from one Domingos Paes, who goes there, and who was at Bisnaga in the time of Crisnarão when Cristovão de Figueiredo was there. I obtained another from Fernão Nuniz, who was there three years trading in horses (which did not prove remunerative). Since one man cannot tell everything—one relating some things which another does not—I send both the summaries made by them, namely, one in the time of Crisnarão, as I have said, and the other sent from there six months since. I desire to do this because your honour can gather what is useful to you from both, and because you will thus give the more credit to some things in the chronicle of the kings of Bisnaga, since they conform one to the other. The copy of the summary which he began to make[1] when he first went to the kingdom of Bisnaga is as follows:—

[1] "He" here is Domingo Paes.

NARRATIVE OF DOMINGOS PAES

(WRITTEN PROBABLY A.D. 1520–22)

OF THE THINGS WHICH I SAW AND CONTRIVED TO LEARN CONCERNING THE KINGDOM OF NARSIMGA, ETC.[1]

ON leaving India[2] to travel towards the kingdom of Narsymga from the sea-coast, you have (first) to pass a range of hills (*serra*), the boundary of the said kingdom and of those territories which are by the sea. This *serra* runs along the whole of the coast of India, and has passes by which people enter the interior; for all the rest of the range is very rocky and is filled with thick forest. The said kingdom has many places on the coast of India; they are seaports with which we are at peace, and in some of them we have factories, namely, Amcola, Mirgeo, Honor, Batecalla, Mamgalor, Bracalor, and Bacanor. And as soon as we are above this *serra* we have a plain country in which there are no more ranges of hills, but only a few mountains, and these small ones; for all the rest is like the plains of Ssantarem.[3] Only on the road from Batecala[4] to a town called *Zambuja*,

[1] The "kingdom of Narsinga" is the name often given by the Portuguese and others to Vijayanagar.

[2] The term here is limited to the small territory of Portuguese India immediately round the city of Goa. Thus Linschoten (A.D. 1583) wrote, "At the end of Cambaya beginneth India, *and* the lands of Decam and Cuncam," meaning that immediately south of the territories of Cambay began those of Portuguese India, while other countries on the border were the Dakhan and the Konkan.

[3] In Portugal.

[4] This was apparently the usual route for travellers from the coast to Vijayanagar. Fr. Luis used it for his journey from Cochin to the capital in 1509 (above, p. 123, and note).

there are some ranges with forests; nevertheless the road is very even. From Batecala to this town of Zambur[1] is forty leagues; the road has many streams of water by its side, and because of this so much merchandise flows to Batecala that every year there come five or six thousand pack-oxen.

Now to tell of the aforesaid kingdom. It is a country sparsely wooded except along this *serra* on the east,[2] but in places you walk for two or three leagues under groves of trees; and behind cities and towns and villages they have plantations of mangoes, and jack-fruit trees, and tamarinds and other very large trees, which form resting-places where merchants halt with their merchandise. I saw in the city of Recalem[3] a tree under which we lodged three hundred and twenty horses, standing in order as in their stables, and all over the country you may see many small trees. These dominions are very well cultivated and very fertile, and are provided with quantities of cattle, such as cows, buffaloes, and sheep; also of birds, both those belonging to the hills and those reared at home, and this in greater abundance than in our tracts. The land has plenty of rice and Indian-corn, grains, beans, and other kind of crops which are not sown in our parts; also an infinity of cotton. Of the grains there is a great quantity, because, besides being used as food for men, it is also used for horses, since there is no other kind of barley; and this country has also much wheat, and that good. The whole country is thickly populated with cities and towns and villages; the king allows them to be surrounded only with earthen walls for fear of their becoming too strong. But if a city is situated at the

1 Probably Sandûr, about 120 miles from the coast at Bhatkal. Sandûr is a small Mahratta state 25 miles from Vijayanagar.

2 That is, on the east of Portuguese India, west of the territory of Vijayanagar.

3 Unidentified. The great tree was of course a banyan.

extremity of his territory he gives his consent to its having stone walls, but never the towns; so that they may make fortresses of the cities but not of the towns.

And because this country is all flat, the winds blow here more than in other parts. The oil which it produces comes from seeds sown and afterwards reaped, and they obtain it by means of machines which they make. This country wants water because it is very great and has few streams; they make lakes in which water collects when it rains, and thereby they maintain themselves. They maintain themselves by means of some in which there are springs better than by others that have only the water from rain; for we find many quite dry, so that people go about walking in their beds, and dig holes to try and find enough water, even a little, for their maintenance. The failure of the water is because they have no winter, as in our parts and in (Portuguese) India, but only thunder-storms that are greater in one year than in another. The water in these lakes is for the most part muddy, especially in those where there are no springs, and the reason why it is so muddy is because of the strong wind and the dust that is in this country, which never allows the water to be clear; and also because of the numbers of cattle, buffaloes, cows, oxen, and other small cattle that drink in them. For you must know that in this land they do not slaughter oxen or cows; the oxen are beasts of burden and are like sumpter-mules; these carry all their goods. They worship the cows, and have them in their pagodas made in stone, and also bulls; they have many bulls that they present to these pagodas, and these bulls go about the city without any one causing them any harm or loss. Further, there are asses in this country, but they are small, and they use them only for little things; those that wash clothes lay the cloths on them, and use them for this more than for anything else. You must know that this kingdom of Narsymga has three hundred *graos* of coast, each *grao* being a league, along the hill-range (*serra*) of which I have spoken, until you arrive at Ballagate and Charamãodel,[1] which belong to this kingdom; and in breadth it is one hundred and sixty-four *graos;* each large *grao* measures two of our leagues, so that it has six hundred leagues of coast, and across it three hundred and forty-eight leagues . . . across from Batacalla to the kingdom of Orya.[2]

And this kingdom marches[3] with all the territory of Bengal, and on the other side with the kingdom of Orya, which is to the east, and on the other side to the north with the kingdom of Dakhan, belonging to which are the lands which the Ydallcão[4] has, and Ozemelluco.[5] Goa is at war with this Ydallcão, because that city was his, and we have taken it from him.

And this kingdom of Orya, of which I have spoken above, is said to be much larger than the kingdom of Narsymga, since it marches with all Bengal, and is at war with her; and it marches with all the kingdom of Pegu and with the *Mallaca* Sea. It reaches to the kingdom of Cambaya; and to the kingdom of Dakhan; and they told me with positive certainty that it extends

[1] Coromandel. This name was applied by the Portuguese to the Eastern Tamil and Southern Telugu countries. It had no well-defined limits, and often was held to extend even as far north as to the Krishnâ river, or even to Orissa. Yule and Burnell adhere to the now generally received definition of the name from *Chola-mandala*, the country of the Cholas (Glossary, *s.v.* Coromandel).

[2] Orissa.

[3] *Comquista com* is evidently an error for *confina com*. The same word is used three times in the next paragraph.

[4] The Âdil Khân, Sultan of Bîjapûr. The name is sometimes written by the Portuguese *Idalxa* (*xa* for *Shâh*). We have numberless spellings in the old chronicles, thus, *Hidalcan*, *Adelham*, &c.

[5] For Nizâm-ul-Mulkh, or the Nizâm Shâh, the Sultan of Ahmadnagar. Similarly the Qutb Shâh of Golkonda is called in these chronicles "Cotamaluco." The Imâd Shâh of Bîrâr is called the "Imademaluco," or even "Madremaluco," by the Dutch (Linschoten) and Portuguese. The Barîd Shâh of Bîdar is styled "Melique Verido."

as far as Persia. The population thereof is light coloured, and the men are of good physique. Its king has much treasure and many soldiers and many elephants, for there are numbers of these in this country. (My informants) know this well, and they say that there is no ruler greater than he. He is a heathen.

Coming back to our subject, I say that I will not mention here the situation of the cities, and towns, and villages in this kingdom of Narsymga, to avoid prolixity; only I shall speak of the city of Darcha,[1] which has a monument such as can seldom be seen elsewhere. This city of Darcha is very well fortified by a wall, though not of stone, for the reason that I have already stated. On the western side, which is towards (Portuguese) India, it is surrounded by a very beautiful river, and on the other, eastern, side the interior of the country is all one plain, and along the wall is its moat. This Darcha has a pagoda, which is the monument I speak of, so beautiful that another as good of its kind could not be found within a great distance. You must know that it is a round temple made of a single stone, the gateway all in the manner of joiners' work, with every art of perspective. There are many figures of the said work, standing out as much as a cubit from the stone, so that you see on every side of them, so well carved that they could not be better done—the faces as well as all the rest; and each one in its place stands as if embowered in leaves; and above it is in the Romanesque style, so well made that it could not be better. Besides this, it has a sort of lesser porch upon pillars, all of stone, and the pillars

[1] The spelling of this name in the original is very doubtful. First it reads *Archa*, on the next occasion it is undoubtedly *Darcha*. The third mention of the place calls it *Larcha*. But in each case the *r* is not very clear, and might be an *i* undotted. Moreover, the *c* may possibly be an *e*, and the name may be *Areha* or *Dareha*. If we should accept the latter, we may identify it with Dhárwár, and believe it to be the same as the *Duree* of Nuniz (below, p. 292).

with their pedestals[1] so well executed that they appear as if made in Italy; all the cross pieces and beams are of the same stone without any planks or timber being used in it, and in the same way all the ground is laid with the same stone, outside as well as in. And all this pagoda, as far round as the temple goes, is enclosed by a trellis made of the same stone, and this again is completely surrounded by a very strong wall, better even than the city has, since it is all of solid masonry. It has three entrance gates, which gates are very large and beautiful, and the entrance from one of these sides, being towards the east and facing the door of the pagoda, has some structures like verandahs, small and low, where sit some *Jogis*;[2] and inside this enclosure, which has other little pagodas of a reddish colour, there is a stone like the mast of a ship, with its pedestal four-sided, and from thence to the top eight-sided, standing in the open air. I was not astonished at it, because I have seen the needle of St. Peter's at Rome, which is as high, or more.[3]

These pagodas are buildings in which they pray and have their idols; the idols are of many sorts, namely, figures of men and women, of bulls, and apes, while others have nothing but a round stone which they worship. In this temple of Darcha is an idol in the figure of a man as to his body, and the face is that of an elephant with trunk and tusks,[4] and with three arms on each side and six hands, of which arms they say that already four are gone, and when all fall then the world will be destroyed; they are full of belief that this will be, and hold it as a prophecy. They feed the idol every day, for they say that he eats; and when he eats women dance before him who belong to that pagoda, and they give him food and all that is necessary, and all girls born of these

[1] *Pranhas* in original, probably for *pianhas* or *peanhas* (see below, p. 288).
[2] *Jogis*, Hindu ascetics.
[3] This probably refers to the Egyptian obelisk at St. Peter's.
[4] Evidently the god *Ganesa*.

Q

women belong to the temple. These women are of loose character, and live in the best streets that there are in the city; it is the same in all their cities, their streets have the best rows of houses. They are very much esteemed, and are classed amongst those honoured ones who are the mistresses of the captains; any respectable man may go to their houses without any blame attaching thereto. These women (are allowed) even to enter the presence of the wives of the king, and they stay with them and eat betel with them, a thing which no other person may do, no matter what his rank may be. This betel is a herb which has a leaf like the leaf of the pepper, or the ivy of our country; they always eat this leaf, and carry it in their mouths with another fruit called areca. This is something like a medlar, but it is very hard, and it is very good for the breath and has many other virtues; it is the best provision for those who do not eat as we do. Some of them eat flesh; they eat all kinds except beef and pork, and yet, nevertheless, they cease not to eat this betel all day.

Afterwards, going from this city of Darcha towards the city of Bisnaga,[1] which is eighteen leagues distant, and is the capital of all the kingdom of Narsymga, where the king always resides, you have many cities and walled villages; and two leagues before you arrive at the city of Bisnaga you have a very lofty *serra* which has passes by which you enter the city. These are called "gates" (*portas*). You must enter by these, for you will have no means of entrance except by them. This range of hills surrounds the city with a circle of twenty-four leagues, and within this range there are others that encircle it

[1] "Bisnaga," the Portuguese rendering of *Vijayanagar*, the "city of victory." The spellings adopted by different writers have been endless. We have Beejanugger and Beejnugger in the translations of Firishtah; Bisnagar, Bidjanagar, Bijanagher, amongst the Portuguese; Bicheneger in the writings of the Russian Nikitin; Bizenegalia in those of the Italian Nicolo dei Conti.

closely. Wherever these ranges have any level ground they cross it with a very strong wall, in such a way that the hills remain all closed, except in the places where the roads come through from the gates in the first range, which are the entrance ways to the city. In such places there are some small pits (or caves?)[1] which could be defended by a few people; these *serras* continue as far as the interior of the city. Between all these enclosures are plains and valleys where rice is grown, and there are gardens with many orange-trees, limes, citrons, and radishes (*rabãos*), and other kinds of garden produce as in Portugal, only not lettuces or cabbages. Between these hill-ranges are many lakes by which they irrigate the crops mentioned, and amongst all these ranges there are no forests or patches of brushwood, except very small ones, nor anything that is green. For these hills are the strangest ever seen, they are of a white stone piled one block over another in manner most singular, so that it seems as if they stood in the air and were not connected one with another; and the city is situated in the middle of these hills and is entirely surrounded by them.

The *serras* reach as far as the kingdom of Daquem,[2] and border upon the territories belonging to the Ydallcão, and upon a city called Rachol that formerly belonged to the king of Narsymga; there has been much war over it, and this king took it from the Ydallcão. So that these ranges are in a way the cause (of the two kingdoms) never uniting and always being at war; and even on the side of Orya also there are ranges, but they are different from these, since like ours they have scrub and small patches of brushwood; these ranges are low and between them are great plains. On the extreme east of these two kingdoms you must know that the country is all covered with scrub, the densest possible to be seen, in

[1] *Buqueyrõis.* The word implies something dug out, as opposed to redoubts, which would be built up.

[2] Dakhan.

which there are great beasts, and (this) forms so strong a fortress for it that it protects both sides; it has its entrances by which they pass from one kingdom to the other. In these passes on the frontier the king of Narsymga has a captain with a quantity of troops, but on the side of (Portuguese) India he has none, except as I have said.

Now turning to the gates of the first range, I say that at the entrance of the gate where those pass who come from Goa, which is the principal entrance on the western side, this king has made within it a very strong city[1] fortified with walls and towers, and the gates at the entrances very strong, with towers at the gates; these walls are not like those of other cities, but are made of very strong masonry such as would be found in few other parts, and inside very beautiful rows of buildings made after their manner with flat roofs. There live in this many merchants, and it is filled with a large population because the king induces many honourable merchants to go there from his cities, and there is much water in it. Besides this the king made a tank[2] there, which, as it seems to me, has the width of a falcon-shot,[3] and it is at the mouth of two hills, so that all the water which comes from either one side or the other collects there; and, besides this, water comes to it from more than three leagues by pipes which run along the lower parts of the range outside. This water is brought from a lake which itself overflows into a little river. The tank has three large pillars handsomely carved with figures; these connect above with certain pipes by which they get water when they have to irrigate their gardens and rice-fields. In order to make this tank the said king broke down a hill which enclosed the

[1] This is Nâgalâpur, the modern Hospett (*Epig. Ind.*, iv. 267).
[2] This tank or lake is described by Nuniz (see p. 364).
[3] *Hũu tiro de fallcão*, a shot from a falcon, an old piece of artillery.

ground occupied by the said tank. In the tank I saw so many people at work that there must have been fifteen or twenty thousand men, looking like ants, so that you could not see the ground on which they walked, so many there were; this tank the king portioned out amongst his captains, each of whom had the duty of seeing that the people placed under him did their work, and that the tank was finished and brought to completion.

The tank burst two or three times, and the king asked his Brahmans to consult their idol as to the reason why it burst so often, and the Brahmans said that the idol was displeased, and desired that they should make a sacrifice, and should give him the blood of men and horses and buffaloes; and as soon as the king heard this he forthwith commanded that at the gate of the pagoda the heads of sixty men should be cut off, and of certain horses and buffaloes, which was at once done.

These Brahmans are like friars with us, and they count them as holy men—I speak of the Brahman priests and the lettered men of the pagodas—because although the king has many Brahmans, they are officers of the towns and cities and belong to the government of them; others are merchants, and others live by their own property and cultivation, and the fruits which grow in their inherited grounds. Those who have charge of the temples are learned men, and eat nothing which suffers death, neither flesh nor fish, nor anything which makes broth red, for they say that it is blood. Some of the other Brahmans whom I mentioned, who seek to serve God, and to do penance, and to live a life like that of the priests, do not eat flesh or fish or any other thing that suffers death, but only vegetables[1] and butter and other things which they make of fruit,[2] with their rice.

[1] *Bredos*, "blites," an insipid kitchen vegetable. But as the word is not common, and as Brahmans make use of most vegetables, I have preferred the more general term.

[2] *Macaas*, literally "apples."

They are all married, and have very beautiful wives; the wives are very retiring, and very seldom leave the house. The women are of light colour, and in the caste of these Brahmans are the fairest men and women that there are in the land; for though there are men in other castes commonly of light complexion, yet these are few. There are many in this country who call themselves Brahmans, but they lead a life very different from those of whom I have spoken, for these last are men to whom the king pays much honour, and he holds them in great favour.

This new city that the king made bears the name of his wife for love of whom he made it,[1] and the said city stands in a plain, and round it the inhabitants make their gardens as the ground suits, each one being separate. In this city the king made a temple with many images. It is a thing very well made, and it has some wells very well made after their fashion; its houses are not built with stories like ours, but are of only one floor, with flat roofs and towers,[2] different from ours, for theirs go from storey to storey. They have pillars, and are all open, with verandahs inside and out, where they can easily put people if they desire, so that they seem like houses belonging to a king. These palaces have an enclosing wall which surrounds them all, and inside are many rows of houses. Before you enter the place where the king is there are two gates with many guards, who prevent any one from entering except the captains and men who have business there; and between these two gates is a very large court with its verandahs round it, where these captains and other honoured people wait till the king summons them to his presence.

This king is of medium height, and of fair com-

[1] It was generally called Nâgalâpur, but Nuniz says that the lady's name was Chinnadevî (below, p. 362).

[2] *Coruchees.* See p. 260, note 3.

plexion and good figure, rather fat than thin; he has on his face signs of small-pox. He is the most feared and perfect king that could possibly be, cheerful of disposition and very merry; he is one that seeks to honour foreigners, and receives them kindly, asking about all their affairs whatever their condition may be He is a great ruler and a man of much justice, but subject to sudden fits of rage,[1] and this is his title—"Crisnarão Macacão,[2] king of kings, lord of the greater lords of India, lord of the three seas and of the land." He has this title[3] because he is by rank a greater lord than any, by reason of what he possesses in (?) armies and territories, but it seems that he has (in fact) nothing compared to what a man like him ought to have, so gallant and perfect is he in all things. This king was constantly at war with the king of Orya, and entered his kingdom, taking and destroying many cities and towns; he put to rout numbers of his soldiers and elephants, and took captive his son, whom he kept for a long time in this city of Bisnaga, where he died; and in order to make a treaty and (preserve) peace, the king of Orya gave him a daughter whom the king of Bisnaga married and has as his wife.

This king has twelve lawful wives, of whom there are three principal ones, the sons of each of these three being heirs of the kingdom, but not those of the others; this is (the case) when there are sons to all of them, but when there is only one son, whosesoever he may be, he is heir. One of these principal wives is the daughter of the king of Orya, and others daughters of a king his vassal who is king of Serimgapatão; another wife is a courtezan whom in his youth he had for mistress before he became king, and she made him

[1] *Grandes supitos.*

[2] A mixture, apparently, of *Mahâ*, "great," and "Shâh."

[3] The passage that follows is not very clear in the original.

promise that if he came to be king he would take her to wife, and thus it came to pass that this courtezan became his wife. For love of her he built this new city, and its name was . . . (*sic in orig.*) . . . Each one of these wives has her house to herself, with her maidens and women of the chamber, and women guards and all other women servants necessary; all these are women, and no man enters where they are, save only the eunuchs, who guard them. These women are never seen by any man, except perhaps by some old man of high rank by favour of the king. When they wish to go out they are carried in litters shut up and closed,[1] so that they cannot be seen, and all the eunuchs with them, fully three or four hundred; and all other people keep a long distance from them. They told us that each of these queens has a very large sum of money and treasure and personal ornaments, namely armlets, bracelets, seed-pearls,[2] pearls and diamonds, and that in great quantity: and they also say that each of them has sixty maidens adorned as richly as could possibly be with many jewels, and rubies and diamonds and pearls and seed-pearls. These we afterwards saw, and stood astonished; we saw them at certain festivals which I will afterwards speak of, and of the manner in which they came. Within, with these maidens, they say that there are twelve thousand women; for you must know that there are women who handle sword

[1] The word last used is *sellados*, literally "sealed."

[2] *Aljofar*. This word is constantly used in the chronicles. Garcia da Orta (*Colloq.* xxxv.) derives it from Cape Julfar in Arabia, near Ormuz. Cobarruvias says it is from Arabic *jauhar*, "jewel" (Yule and Burnell, Dict.). Da Orta writes: "*Chama-se* perla *em castelhano e* perola *em portuguez, e em latim* unio, *e isto no* aljofar *grande; porque o miudo chama-se em latim* margarita, *e em arabio* lulu, *e em persio e nest' outras gerações da India* moti, *e em malavar* mutu, *e em portuguez e castelhano* aljofar;" *i.e.* a large pearl is called *perla* in Spanish, *perola* in Portuguese, *unio* in Latin; a small pearl is called in Latin *margarita*, in Arabic *lulu*, in Persian and many Indian languages *moti*, in Malayâlam *mutu*, and in Portuguese and Spanish *aljofar*.

and shield, and others who wrestle, and others who blow trumpets, and others pipes, and others instruments which are different from ours; and in the same way they have women as bearers (*boois*) and washing-folk, and for other offices inside their gates, just as the king has the officers of his household. These three principal wives have each the same, one as much as the other, so that there may never be any discord or ill feeling between them; all of them are great friends, and each one lives by herself. It may be gathered from this what a large enclosure there must be for these houses where so many people live, and what streets and lanes they must have.

The king lives by himself inside the palace, and when he wishes to have with him one of his wives he orders a eunuch to go and call her. The eunuch does not enter where she is, but tells it to the female guards, who make known to the queen that there is a message from the king, and then comes one of her maidens or chamber-women and learns what is wanted, and then the queen goes where the king is, or the king comes where she is, and so passes the time as it seems good to him without any of the others knowing. Amongst these eunuchs the king has some who are great favourites, and who sleep where he sleeps; they receive a large salary.

This king is accustomed every day to drink a *quartilho* (three-quarter pint) of oil of *gingelly*[1] before daylight, and anoints himself all over with the said oil; he covers his loins with a small cloth, and takes in his arms great weights made of earthenware, and then, taking a sword, he exercises himself with it till he has sweated out all the oil, and then he wrestles with one of his wrestlers. After this labour he mounts a horse

[1] *Emgellym*, sesamum or gingelly, an oil seed.

and gallops about the plain in one direction and another till dawn, for he does all this before daybreak. Then he goes to wash himself, and a Brahman washes him whom he holds sacred, and who is a great favourite of his and is a man of great wealth; and after he is washed he goes to where his pagoda is inside the palace, and makes his orisons and ceremonies, according to custom. Thence he goes to a building made in the shape of a porch without walls, which has many pillars hung with cloths right up to the top, and with the walls handsomely painted; it has on each side two figures of women very well made. In such a building he despatches his work with those men who bear office in his kingdom, and govern his cities, and his favourites talk with them. The greatest favourite is an old man called Temersea;[1] he commands the whole household, and to him all the great lords act as to the king. After the king has talked with these men on subjects pleasing to him he bids enter the lords and captains who wait at the gate, and these at once enter to make their salaam to him. As soon as they appear they make their salaam to him, and place themselves along the walls far off from him; they do not speak one to another, nor do they chew betel before him, but they place their hands in the sleeves of their tunics (*cabayas*) and cast their eyes on the ground; and if the king desires to speak to any one it is done through a second person, and then he to whom the king desires to speak raises his eyes and replies to him who questions him, and then returns to his former position. So they remain till the king bids them go, and then they all turn to make the salaam to him and go out. The salaam,

[1] This was the great Sâluva Timma, Krishna Deva's minister. The termination *-rsea* probably represents *Arasa*, the Kanarese form for *Râjah*. *Temersea = Timmarasa = Timma Râjah.*

which is the greatest courtesy that exists among them, is that they put their hands joined above their head as high as they can. Every day they go to make the salaam to the king.

When we came to this country the king was in this new town, and there went to see him Christovão de Figueiredo[1] with all of us Portuguese that came with him, and all very handsomely dressed after our manner, with much finery; the king received him very well, and was very complacent to him. The king was as much pleased with him as if he had been one of his own people, so much attention did he evince towards him; and also towards those amongst us who went with him he showed much kindness. We were so close to the king that he touched us all and could not have enough of looking at us. Then Christovão de Figueiredo gave him the letters from the Captain-Major[2] and the things he had brought for him, with which he was greatly delighted; principally with certain organs[3] that the said Christovão de Figueiredo brought him, with many other things (*peças*). The king was clothed in certain white cloths embroidered with many roses in gold, and

[1] According to Correa, Christovão de Figueiredo had been sent by the governor, Lopo Soares, in 1517 to Vijayanagar as factor, with horses and elephants (*Lendas da India*, ii. 509–510); but Senhor Lopes points out (Introduction to his *Chronica*, lxxxii. note) that we do not know how far this assertion is true. He certainly lived at Goa, and not long after this battle was made chief *Tanedar* of the mainlands of Goa, with residence at the temple of Mardor. He was several times in peril at the hands of the Mussalmâns, and in 1536 was present at the battles which took place between the Portuguese and Asada Khân of Belgaum, with whom he was on terms of friendship. Mr. Danvers (ii. 507) states that he was also at one time attorney of the factory of Goa.

[2] This apparently refers to Ruy de Mello (see above, p. 142 ff.). If De Sequeira were meant he would have been called "Governor."

[3] *Horgãos*. Mr. Ferguson points out that these were undoubtedly musical instruments. Castanheda (v. xxviii.), describing the embassy to "Prester John" under Dom Roderigo de Lima in 1520 (the same year), states that among the presents sent to that potentate were "some organs and a clavichord, and a player for them." These organs are also mentioned in Father Alvares's account of their embassy (Hakluyt Society Trans., p. 10).

with a *pateca*[1] of diamonds on his neck of very great value, and on his head he had a cap of brocade in fashion like a Galician helmet, covered with a piece of fine stuff all of fine silk, and he was barefooted; for no one ever enters where the king is unless he has bare feet, and the majority of the people, or almost all, go about the country barefooted. The shoes have pointed ends, in the ancient manner, and there are other shoes that have nothing but soles, but on top are some straps which help to keep them on the feet. They are made like those which of old the Romans were wont to wear, as you will find on figures in some papers or antiquities which come from Italy. The king gave to Christovão de Figueiredo on dismissing him a *cabaya* (tunic) of brocade, with a cap of the same fashion as the king wore,[2] and to each one of the Portuguese he gave a cloth embroidered with many pretty figures, and this the king gives because it is customary; he gives it in token of friendship and love.

When Christovão de Figueiredo had been dismissed by the king we came to the city of Bisnaga, which is a league from this new city, and here he commanded us to be lodged in some very good houses; and Figueiredo was visited by many lords and captains, and other persons who came on behalf of the king. And the king sent him many sheep and fowls, and many vessels (*calões*) full of butter and honey and many other things to eat, which he at once distributed amongst all the foot-soldiers and people whom he had brought with him. The king said many kind and pleasant things to him, and asked him concerning the kind of state which

[1] *Pateca*, something worn round the neck. There appears to be some mistake here, as *pateca* means "a sort of long robe or gown (worn) in India" (Michaelis' Dict.).

[2] Varthema says, "The king wears a cap of gold brocade two spans long." This was Krishna Deva's predecessor, Narasimha.

the king of Portugal kept up; and having been told about it all he seemed much pleased.

Returning then to the city of Bisnaga, you must know that from it to the new city goes a street as wide as a place of tourney, with both sides lined throughout with rows of houses and shops where they sell everything; and all along this road are many trees that the king commanded to be planted, so as to afford shade to those that pass along. On this road he commanded to be erected a very beautiful temple of stone,[1] and there are other pagodas that the captains and great lords caused to be erected.

So that, returning to the city of Bisnaga, you must know that before you arrive at the city gates there is a gate with a wall that encloses all the other enclosures of the city, and this wall is a very strong one and of massive stonework; but at the present time it is injured in some places. They do not fail to have citadels[2] in it. This wall has a moat of water in some places, and in the parts where it was constructed on low ground. And there is, separate from it, yet another (defence) made in the following manner. Certain pointed stones of great height are fixed in the ground as high as a man's breast; they are in breadth a lance-shaft and a half, with the same distance between them and the great wall. This wall rises in all the low ground till it reaches some hill or rocky land. From this first circuit until you enter the city there is a great distance, in which are fields in which they sow rice and have many gardens and much water, which water comes from two lakes. The water passes through this first line of wall, and there is much water in the lakes

[1] This may refer to the handsome temple of Anantasâyana, a mile or so from Hospett on the road to Kâmalâpur. The trees still stand in parts.

[2] *Fortalezas.* Probably the writer refers either to bastions or towers, or to strongly fortified places of refuge on the hilltops. The passage is obscure.

because of springs; and here there are orchards and a little grove of palms, and many houses.

Returning, then, to the first gate of the city, before you arrive at it you pass a little piece of water and then you arrive at the wall, which is very strong, all of stone-work, and it makes a bend before you arrive at the gate; and at the entrance of this gate are two towers, one on each side, which makes it very strong. It is large and beautiful. As soon as you pass inside there are two little temples; one of them has an enclosing wall with many trees, while the whole of the other consists of buildings; and this wall of the first gate encircles the whole city. Then going forward you have another gate with another line of wall, and it also encircles the city inside the first, and from here to the king's palace is all streets and rows of houses, very beautiful, and houses of captains and other rich and honourable men; you will see rows of houses with many figures and decorations pleasing to look at. Going along the principal street, you have one of the chief gateways,[1] which issues from a great open space[2] in front of the king's palace; opposite this is another which passes along to the other side of the city; and across this open space pass all the carts and conveyances carrying stores and everything else, and because it is in the middle of the city it cannot but be useful.

This palace of the king is surrounded by a very strong wall like some of the others, and encloses a greater space (*teraa moor cerca*) than all the castle of Lisbon.

Still going forward, passing to the other gate you see two temples connected with it, one on each side,

[1] Four words, *temdes hũa porta primcipal*, have been accidentally omitted in the printed copy.

[2] *Terreiro.* The gateway here spoken of is most probably the great entrance to the palace enclosure, just to the north of the village of Kâmalâpur.

CORNER OF A PAVILION, SHOWING REMAINS OF STREET AT VIJAYANAGAR

(*From a Photograph by* Col. W. Hooper)

and at the door of one of these they kill every day many sheep; for in all the city they do not kill any sheep for the use of the heathen (Hindus), or for sale in the markets, except at the gate of this pagoda. Of their blood they make sacrifices to the idol that is in the temple. They leave the heads to him, and for each sheep they give a *saco* (*chakram*), which is a coin like a *cartilha* (*quartilha*—a farthing).

There is present at the slaughter of these beasts a *jogi* (priest) who has charge of the temple, and as soon as they cut off the head of the sheep or goat this *jogi* blows a horn as a sign that the idol receives that sacrifice. Hereafter I shall tell of these *jogis*, what sort of men they are.[1]

Close to these pagodas is a triumphal car covered with carved work and images, and on one day in each year during a festival they drag this through the city in such streets as it can traverse. It is large and cannot turn corners.

Going forward, you have a broad and beautiful street, full of rows of fine houses and streets of the sort I have described, and it is to be understood that the houses belong to men rich enough to afford such. In this street live many merchants, and there you will find all sorts of rubies, and diamonds, and emeralds, and pearls, and seed-pearls, and cloths, and every other sort of thing there is on earth and that you may wish to buy. Then you have there every evening a fair where they sell many common horses and nags (*rocis e semdeiros*), and also many citrons, and limes, and oranges, and grapes, and every other kind of garden stuff, and wood; you have all in this street. At the end of it you have another gate with its wall, which wall goes to meet the wall of the second gate of which I have spoken, in such sort that

[1] The writer forgot to fulfil this promise.

this city has three fortresses, with another which is the king's palace. Then when this gate is passed you have another street where there are many craftsmen, and they sell many things; and in this street there are two small temples. There are temples in every street, for these appertain to institutions like the confraternities you know of in our parts,[1] of all the craftsmen and merchants; but the principal and greatest pagodas are outside the city. In this street lodged Christovão de Figueiredo. On every Friday you have a fair there, with many pigs and fowls and dried fish from the sea, and other things the produce of the country, of which I do not know the name; and in like manner a fair is held every day in different parts of the city. At the end of this street is the Moorish quarter, which is at the very end of the city, and of these Moors there are many who are natives of the country[2] and who are paid by the king and belong to his guard. In this city you will find men belonging to every nation and people, because of the great trade which it has, and the many precious stones there, principally diamonds.

The size of this city I do not write here, because it cannot all be seen from any one spot, but I climbed a hill whence I could see a great part of it; I could not see it all because it lies between several ranges of hills. What I saw from thence seemed to me as large as Rome, and very beautiful to the sight; there are many groves of trees within it, in the gardens of the houses, and many conduits of water which flow into the midst of it, and in places there are lakes (*tamques*); and the king has close to his palace a palm-grove and other rich-bearing fruit-trees. Below the Moorish quarter is a little river, and on this side are many

[1] *Por que são como as comfraryas que nas nossas partes haa.*
[2] *A muytos naturaes da terra.*

orchards and gardens with many fruit-trees, for the most part mangoes and areca-palms and jack-trees, and also many lime and orange trees, growing so closely one to another that it appears like a thick forest; and there are also white grapes. All the water which is in the city comes from the two tanks of which I have spoken, outside the first enclosing wall.

The people in this city are countless in number, so much so that I do not wish to write it down for fear it should be thought fabulous; but I declare that no troops, horse or foot, could break their way through any street or lane, so great are the numbers of the people and elephants.

This is the best provided city in the world, and is stocked with provisions such as rice, wheat, grains, Indian-corn, and a certain amount of barley and beans, *moong*,[1] pulses, horse-gram,[2] and many other seeds which grow in this country which are the food of the people, and there is large store of these and very cheap; but wheat is not so common as the other grains, since no one eats it except the Moors. But you will find what I have mentioned. The streets and markets are full of laden oxen without count, so that you cannot get along for them, and in many streets you come upon so many of them that you have to wait for them to pass, or else have to go by another way. There is much poultry; they give three fowls in the city for a coin worth a *vintem*,[3] which coins are called *favaos*;[4] outside the city they give four fowls for a *vintem*.

In this country there are many partridges, but

[1] *Munguo.* "Moong . . . green gram . . . a kind of vetch" (Yule and Burnell, Dict.).

[2] *Macharuy.*

[3] A *vintem* = 1 $\frac{7}{20}$ of a penny.

[4] Probably for *fanaos*. But the plural of *fanao* is usually given as *fanões*.

R

they are not of the same sort or quality as ours: they are like the *estarnas*[1] of Italy.

There are three sorts of these: one class has only a small spur such as those of Portugal have; another class has on each foot two very sharp spurs, almost as long and thick as one's finger; the other class is painted, and of these you will find the markets full; as also of quails, and hares, and all kinds of wild fowl, and other birds which live in the lakes and which look like geese. All these birds and game animals they sell alive, and they are very cheap, for they give six or eight partridges for a *vintem*, and of hares they give two and sometimes one. Of other birds they give more than you can count, for even of the large ones they give so many that you would hardly pay any attention to the little ones they give you, such as doves and pigeons and the common birds of the country. The doves are of two kinds; some are like those in Portugal, others are as large as thrushes; of the doves they give twelve or fourteen for a *favao;* the pigeons are the same price as the other birds. Then the sheep that they kill every day are countless, one could not number them, for in every street there are men who will sell you mutton, so clean and so fat that it looks like pork; and you also have pigs in some streets of butchers' houses so white and clean that you could never see better in any country; a pig is worth four or five *fanams*.[2] Then to see the many loads of limes that come each day, such that those of Povos are of no account,[3] and also loads of sweet and sour oranges, and wild *brinjals*, and other garden stuff in such abundance as to stupefy one. For the state of this city is not like

[1] *Estarna.* "A sort of small partridge with black feet" (Michaelis' Dict.).
[2] Here we have the plural *fanõees*.
[3] Povos is a place near Lisbon.

that of other cities, which often fail of supplies and provisions, for in this one everything abounds; and also the quantity of butter and oil and milk sold every day, that is a thing I cannot refrain from mentioning; and as for the rearing of cows and buffaloes which goes on in the city, there is so much that you will go very far before you find another like it. There are many pomegranates also; grapes are sold at three bunches a *fanam*, and pomegranates ten for a *fanam*.

On the north side of the city is a very great river with much water, in which are many fish, which fish are very unwholesome, and in this river there is that which passes for . . . (*sic. in orig.*); other streams flow into it, which make it very large.

Now as to the places on the bank of this river. There is a city built there which they call *Senagumdym*,[1] and they say that of old it was the capital of the kingdom, but there now live in it few people; it still has good walls and is very strong, and it lies between two hill-ranges which have only two entrances. A captain lives in this city for the king. People cross to this place by boats which are round like baskets;[2] inside they are made of cane, and outside are covered with leather; they are able to carry fifteen or twenty persons, and even horses and oxen can cross in them if necessary, but for the most part these animals swim across. Men row them with a sort of paddle, and the boats are always turning round, as they cannot go straight like others; in all the kingdom where there are streams there are no other boats but these.[3]

There are also in this city places where they sell live sheep; you will see the fields round the city full of them.

[1] Ânegundi.

[2] Below, pp. 292, 293.

[3] The stone bridge, built on rows of rough monolithic uprights, the remains of which are still to be seen near the temple of Vitthalasvâmi, appears, from the absence of allusion to it, to have been constructed at a later date.

and also of cows and buffaloes—it is a very pretty sight to see,—and also the many she-goats and kids, and the he-goats so large that they are bridled and saddled. Many sheep are like that also, and boys ride them.

Outside the city walls on the north there are three very beautiful pagodas, one of which is called *Vitella*,[1] and it stands over against this city of Nagumdym; the other is called *Aŏperadianar*,[2] and this is the one which they hold in most veneration, and to which they make great pilgrimages.

In this pagoda, opposite to its principal gate which is to the east, there is a very beautiful street of very beautiful houses with balconies and arcades, in which are sheltered the pilgrims that come to it, and there are also houses for the lodging of the upper classes; the king has a palace in the same street, in which he resides when he visits this pagoda. There is a pomegranate tree[3] above this first gate; the gate has a very lofty tower all covered with rows of men and women and hunting scenes and many other representations, and as the tower goes narrowing towards the top so the images diminish in size. Passing this first gate, you come at once into a large courtyard with another gate of the same sort as the first, except that it is rather smaller throughout; and passing this second gate, there is a large court with verandahs all round on pillars of

[1] This clearly alludes to the beautifully sculptured temple of Vitthalasvâmi, which is in the situation described.

[2] This word is a puzzle. If the temple be, as seems most probable from the description, the principal temple at Hampe, still in use, I suggest that *Aôpe* represents "Hampi" or "Hampe." *Radi* may be "râjah," or *radian* may be "râjyam." The name was perhaps given to Paes by some one who described it as "the royal Hampe temple," and this would accurately describe it. It was dedicated to Virûpâksha, and was the cathedral of the great city.

[3] The word used is *romeyra*, which may mean either a pomegranate tree or a female pilgrim. The allusion is to the plaster figures and designs on the tower (*corucheo*) above the gate.

ONE OF THE PAVILIONS IN THE TEMPLE OF VITTHALASVAMI

(*From a Photograph by* F. DUNSTERVILLE, Esq.)

stone, and in the middle of this court is the house of the idol.

Opposite the principal gate stand four columns, two gilded and the other two copper, from which, owing to their great age as it seems to me, the gold has worn off; and the other two are also of copper, for all are of copper. That which stands nearest the gate of the temple was given by this King Crisnarão who now reigns here, and the others by his predecessors. All the outer side of the gate of the temple up to the roof is covered with copper and gilded, and on each side of the roof on the top are certain great animals that look like tigers, all gilt. As soon as you enter this idol-shrine, you perceive from pillar to pillar on which it is supported many little holes in which stand oil lamps, which burn, so they tell me, every night, and they will be in number two thousand five hundred or three thousand lights. As soon as you pass this shrine you enter another small one like the crypt (*cinzeyro*)[1] of some church; it has two doors at the sides, and thence onward this building is like a chapel, where stands the idol which they adore. Before you get to it there are three doors; the shrine is vaulted and dark without any light from the sky; it is always lit with candles. At the first gate are doorkeepers who never allow any one to enter except the Brahmans that have charge of it, and I, because I gave something to them, was allowed to enter. Between gate and gate are images of little idols. The principal idol is a round stone without any shape; they have great devotion for it. This building outside is all covered with copper gilt. At the back of the temple outside, close to the verandahs of which I have spoken, there is a small idol of white

[1] *Cinzeyro* apparently means a place for ashes (*cinza*). *Cinzas* are "ashes of the dead." The reference may be to a place in a church where incense-burners are kept, or, as I think, equally well to the crypt, and this last sense seems better to suit the context.

alabaster with six arms;[1] in one it has a . . .[2] and in the other a sword, and in the others sacred emblems (*armas de casa*), and it has below its feet a buffalo, and a large animal which is helping to kill that buffalo. In this pagoda there burns continually a lamp of *ghee*, and around are other small temples for houses of devotion.

The other temples aforesaid are made in the same manner, but this one is the principal one and the oldest; they all have many buildings and gardens with many trees, in which the Brahmans cultivate their vegetables[3] and the other herbs that they eat. Whenever the festival of any of these temples occurs they drag along certain triumphal cars which run on wheels, and with it go dancing-girls and other women with music to the temple, (conducting) the idol along the said street with much pomp. I do not relate the manner in which these cars are taken, because in all the time that I was in this city none were taken round. There are many other temples in the city of which I do not here speak, to avoid prolixity.

You should know that among these heathen there are days when they celebrate their feasts as with us; and they have their days of fasting, when all day they eat nothing, and eat only at midnight. When the time of the principal festival arrives the king comes from the new city to this city of Bisnaga, since it is the capital of the kingdom and it is the custom there to make their feasts and to assemble. For these feasts are summoned all the dancing-women of the kingdom, in order that they should be present; and also the captains and kings and great lords with all their retinues,—except only those whom the king may have sent to make war, or those who are in other parts, or at the far end of the kingdom

[1] *Seus* for *seis*.
[2] The word is omitted in the original.
[3] *Bredos*. See above, pp. 227, 245, notes.

on the side where (an attack) is feared, such as the kingdom of Oria and the territories of the Ydallcão; and even if such captains are absent in such places, there appear for them at the feasts those whom I shall hereafter mention.

These feasts begin on the 12th of September,[1] and they last nine days, and take place at the king's palace.

The palace is on this fashion: it has a gate opening on to the open space[2] of which I have spoken, and over this gate is a tower of some height, made like the others with its verandahs; outside these gates begins the wall which I said encircled the palace. At the gate are many doorkeepers[3] with leather scourges in their hands, and sticks, and they let no one enter but the captains and chief people, and those about whom they receive orders from the Chief of the Guard. Passing this gate you have an open space, and then you have another gate like the first, also with its doorkeepers and guards; and as soon as you enter inside this you have a large open space, and on one side and the other are low verandahs where are seated the captains and chief people in order to witness the feasts, and on the left side of the north of this open space is a great one-storeyed building (*terrea*); all the rest are like it. This building stands on pillars shaped like elephants and with other figures, and all open in front, and they go up to it by staircases of stone; around it, underneath, is a terrace (*corredor*) paved with very good flagstones, where stand some of the people looking at the feast. This house is called the House of Victory, as it was made when the king came back from the war against Orya, as I have already told you. On the right side of the open space were some

[1] For a discussion as to the dates given in Paes, see p. 140 ff. above.

[2] *Terreyro*. See above, p. 254. Evidently the place of arms is referred to.

[3] *Porteyros*, *Porteyro moor*. These men are often mentioned in the chronicle. Their chief was one of the king's most important officers, and I give him the title "Chief of the Guard."

narrow scaffoldings, made of wood and so lofty that they could be seen over the top of the wall; they were covered at the top with crimson and green velvet and other handsome cloths, and adorned from top to bottom. Let no one fancy that these cloths were of wool, because there are none such in the country, but they are of very fine cotton. These scaffoldings are not always kept at that place, but they are specially made for these feasts; there are eleven of them. Against the gates there were two circles in which were the dancing-women, richly arrayed with many jewels of gold and diamonds and many pearls. Opposite the gate which is on the east side of the front of the open space, and in the middle of it, there are two buildings of the same sort as the House of Victory of which I have spoken; these buildings are served by a kind of staircase of stone beautifully wrought,—one is in the middle and the other at the end. This building was all hung with rich cloths, both the walls and the ceiling, as well as the supports, and the cloths of the walls were adorned with figures in the manner of embroidery; these buildings have two platforms one above the other, beautifully sculptured, with their sides well made and worked, to which platforms the sons of the king's favourites come for the feasts, and sometimes his eunuchs. On the upper platform, close to the king, was Christovão de Figueiredo, with all of us who came with him, for the king commanded that he should be put in such a place as best to see the feasts and magnificence. That I may not forget to tell of the streets that are in the palace I here mention them. You must know that inside the palace that I have spoken of is the dwelling of the king and of his wives and of the other women who serve them, as I have already said, who are twelve thousand in number; and they have an entrance to these rows of houses so that they can go inside. Between this palace and the House of Victory is a gate which serves as passage to it. Inside there are thirty-four streets.

Returning to the feasts, you must know that in this House of Victory the king has a room (*casa*) made of cloth, with its door closed, where the idol has a shrine; and in the other, in the middle (of the building), is placed a daïs opposite the staircase in the middle; on which daïs stands a throne of state made thus,—it is four-sided, and flat, with a round top, and a hollow in the middle for the seat. As regards the woodwork of it, you must know that it is all covered with silk cloths (? *soajes*),[1] and has lions all of gold, and in the spaces between the cloths (*soajes*) it has plates of gold with many rubies and seed-pearls, and pearls underneath; and round the sides it is all full of golden images of personages, and upon these is much work in gold, with many precious stones. In this chair is placed an idol, also of gold, embowered in roses and flowers. On one side of this chair, on the daïs below, stands a head-dress; this also is made in the same manner; it is upright and as high as a span, the top is rounded, it is all full of pearls and rubies and all other precious stones, and on the top of it is a pearl as large as a nut, which is not quite round. On the other side is an anklet for the foot made in the same fashion; it is another state jewel, and is full of large pearls and of many rubies, emeralds, and diamonds, and other stones of value; it will be of the thickness of a man's arm. In front of all this, at the edge[2] of the daïs, resting on a support were some cushions where the king was seated during all these feasts. The feasts commence thus:—

---

[1] I am doubtful about this translation. The word used has probably some technical meaning. Yule's Dictionary has *soosie* from Persian *súsí*. "Some kind of silk cloth, but we know not what kind." The original passage runs:—"Quoanto ao pao, sabereis que he toda chea de suas soajes, e de liõis todos d ouro, e no vão d estas soajes tem hũas chapas d ouro com muytos robis," &c.

[2] *Cabo*. I think this must mean the edge, the front, not the extreme end of the king's balcony.

You must know that when it is morning the king comes to this House of Victory, and betakes himself to that room where the idol is with its Brahmans, and he performs his prayers and ceremonies. Outside the house are some of his favourites, and on the square are many dancing-girls dancing. In their verandahs round the square are many captains and chief people who come there in order to see; and on the ground, near the platform of the house, are eleven horses with handsome and well-arranged trappings, and behind them are four beautiful elephants with many adornments. After the king has entered inside he comes out, and with him a Brahman who takes in his hand a basket full of white roses and approaches the king on the platform, and the king, taking three handfuls of these roses, throws them to the horses,[1] and after he has thrown them he takes a basket of perfumes and acts towards them as though he would cense them; and when he has finished doing this he reaches towards the elephants and does the same to them. And when the king has finished this, the Brahman takes the basket and descends to the platform,[2] and from thence puts those roses and other flowers on the heads of all the horses, and this done, returns to the king. Then the king goes again to where the idol is, and as soon as he is inside they lift the curtains[3] of the room, which are made like the purdahs of a tent, and the king seats himself there where these are, and they lift them all. Thence he witnesses the slaughter of twenty-four buffaloes and a hundred and fifty sheep, with which a sacrifice is made to that idol; you must know that they cut off the heads of these buffaloes and sheep at one blow with certain large sickles which are

[1] This is given in the singular number, probably by mistake, as the plural is used immediately afterwards—*ao cavallo . . . os encemça.*

[2] *Tavoleiro.*

[3] *Paredes*, probably for "purdahs" (Persian, *parda*), curtains or screens. The Portuguese word means a "wall."

wielded by a man who has charge of this slaughter; they are so sure of hand that no blow misses. When they have finished the slaughter of these cattle the king goes out and goes to the other large buildings, on the platforms of which is a crowd of Brahmans, and as soon as the king ascends to where they stand they throw to the king ten or twelve roses—those (that is) who are nearest to him. Then he passes all along the top of the buildings, and as soon as he is at the end he takes the cap from his head, and after placing it on the ground turns back (to the place) where the idol is; here he lies extended on the ground. When he has arisen he betakes himself to the interior of the building, and enters a garden (or walled enclosure—*quyntal*) where they say that a little fire has been made, and he throws into the fire a powder made up of many things, namely, rubies and pearls and all other kinds of precious stones, and aloes and other sweet-scented things. This done, he returns to the pagoda and goes inside and stays a little, at which time enter by the other door some of his favourites who are in the building, and they make their salaam. Then he goes back to the place whence he threw the flowers to the horses, and as soon as he is here all the captains and chief people come and make their salaam to him, and some, if they so desire, present some gifts to him; then as they came so they retire, and each one betakes himself to his own dwelling. And the king withdraws to the interior of his palace by that gate which I have already mentioned—that which stands between the two buildings that are in the arena (*terreyro*); the courtesans and bayadères[1] remain dancing in front of the temple and idol for a long time. This is what is done during the morning of each day of these nine days, with the ceremonies I have

[1] *Molheres solteiras e baylhadeiras*, *i.e.* the dancing-girls of the temple and palace.

mentioned, and each day more splendid (than the last).

Now, returning to the feasts. At three o'clock in the afternoon every one comes to the palace. They do not admit every one at once (they allowed us to go into the open part that is between the gates), but there go inside only the wrestlers and dancing-women, and the elephants, which go with their trappings and decorations, those that sit on them being armed with shields and javelins, and wearing quilted tunics.[1] As soon as these are inside they range themselves round the arena, each one in his place, and the wrestlers go close to the staircase which is in the middle of that building, where has been prepared a large space of ground for the dancing-women to wrestle. Many other people are then at the entrance-gate opposite to the building, namely Brahmans, and the sons of the king's favourites, and their relations; all these are noble youths who serve before the king. The officers of the household go about keeping order amongst all the people, and keep each one in his own place. The different pavilions are separated by doors, so that no one may enter unless he is invited.

Salvatinica,[2] who is the principal person that enters the building, supervises the whole, for he brought up the king and made him king, and so the king looks on him like a father. Whenever the king calls to him he addresses him as "Lord (*senhor*) Salvatinica," and all the captains and nobles of the realm make salaam to him. This Salvatinica stands inside the arena where the festivals go on, near one of the doors, and from there gives the word for the admission of all the things necessary for the festival.

[1] *Lavodes.* See below, p. 276, note regarding *laudes.*

[2] Sâluva Timma, the minister. The name is spelt in various ways in the chronicles of both Paes and Nuniz. Krishna Deva owed his throne to him (below, p. 315).

RUINS OF "HOUSE OF VICTORY" AT THE PALACE, VIJAYANAGAR

After all this is done and arranged the king goes forth and seats himself on the daïs I have mentioned, where is the throne and the other things, and all those that are inside make their salaam to him. As soon as they have done this the wrestlers seat themselves on the ground, for these are allowed to remain seated, but no other, howsoever great a lord he be, except the king so commands; and these also eat betel, though none else may eat it in his presence except the dancing-women, who may always eat it before him. As soon as the king is seated in his place he bids to sit with him three or four men who belong to his race, and who are themselves kings and the fathers of his wives; the principal of these is the king of Syrimgapatão and of all the territory bordering on Malabar, and this king is called Cumarvirya,[1] and he seats himself as far in front as the king on the other side of the daïs, the rest are behind.

There the king sits, dressed in white clothes all covered with (embroidery of) golden roses and wearing his jewels—he wears a quantity of these white garments, and I always saw him so dressed—and around him stand his pages with his betel, and his sword, and the other things which are his insignia of state. Many Brahmans stand round the throne on which rests the idol, fanning it with horsetail plumes, coloured, the handles of which

[1] The king of Seringapatam at this period was Bettâda Châma Râya, who ruled the Mysore country from 1513 to 1552. He had three sons. The two eldest received at his death portions of his estate, but both died without issue. The third son was called "Hîre" or "Vîra" Châma. He was apparently the most powerful, and the best beloved of his father, since he received as his portion on the latter's death the principal tract of Mysore, the town itself, and the neighbouring province. After the fall of Vijayanagar in 1565 he became practically independent, and ruled till the principal power was seized by his relative, Râja Udaiyâr, in 1578. The word *Kumâra* (= "son") is often applied in royal families in India to one of the reigning king's offspring, and I venture to think that *Cumarvirya* represents *Kumâra Vîrayya*, the king of Seringapatam being himself not present at these feasts, and the personage seen by Paes being his son Vîra.

are all overlaid with gold; these plumes are tokens of the highest dignity; they also fan the king with them.

As[1] soon as the king is seated, the captains who waited without make their entrance, each one by himself, attended by his chief people, and so on, all in order; they approach and make their salaams to the king, and then take their places in the pavilions (*veramdas*) which I have previously described. As soon as these nobles have finished entering, the captains of the troops approach with shields and spears, and afterwards the captains of the archers; these officers are all stationed on the ground around the arena in front of the elephants, and they constitute the king's guard, for into such a place no man may enter bearing arms, nor near to where the king is. As soon as these soldiers have all taken their places the women begin to dance, while some of them place themselves in the circular galleries that I have said were (erected) at their gate of entrance. Who can fitly describe to you the great riches these women carry on their persons?—collars of gold with so many diamonds and rubies and pearls, bracelets also on their arms and on their upper arms, girdles below, and of necessity anklets on the feet. The marvel should be otherwise, namely that women of such a profession should obtain such wealth; but there are women among them who have lands that have been given to them, and litters, and so many maid-servants that one cannot number all their things. There is a woman in this city who is said to have a hundred thousand *pardaos*,[2] and I believe this from what I have seen of them.

[1] The writer begins again, "But returning to the feasts." I have omitted the phrase here, as it has become rather monotonous.

[2] A small gold coin, of which it is very difficult to assess the exact value. Abdur Razzâk (1443) apparently makes it equal to the half pagoda; Varthema (1503–7) to the pagoda itself; and this latter is the sense in which we must take it. Varthema calls it a "gold ducat." Purchas says it was in

Then the wrestlers begin their play. Their wrestling does not seem like ours, but there are blows (given), so severe as to break teeth, and put out eyes, and disfigure faces, so much so that here and there men are carried off speechless by their friends; they give one another fine falls too. They have their captains and judges, who are there to put each one on an equal footing in the field, and also to adjust the honours to him who wins.

In all this portion of the day nothing more is done than this wrestling and the dancing of the women, but as soon as ever the sun is down many torches are lit and some great flambeaux made of cloth; and these are placed about the arena in such a way that the whole is as light as day, and even along the top of the walls, for on all the battlements are lighted lamps, and the place where the king sits is all full of torches. As soon as these are all lit up there are introduced many very graceful plays and contrivances, but these do not stop long; they only approach where the king is and then go out. Then there enter others in other fashion, with battles of people on horseback; these horses are like the hobby-horses made in Portugal for the feast of the Corpo de Dios; others come with casting-nets, fishing, and capturing the men that are in the arena. When these amusements are ended, they begin to throw up many rockets and many different sorts of fires, also castles that burn and fling out from themselves many bombs (*tiros*) and rockets.

When these fireworks are finished, there enter many triumphal cars which belong to the captains, some of

his day about the value of a Flemish dollar. The general value assigned in more recent days to the pagoda is 3½ rupees, or seven shillings when the rupee stands at par value. (See Yule and Burnell's Dictionary, "Hobson-Jobson," *s.v.* "pagoda" and "pardao." Yule apparently values it, at the period treated of, as about 4s. 6d.) Barros and Castanheda both agree with Paes that the pardao was worth 360 reis. (Below, p. 282.)

them sent by those captains who are waging war in foreign parts; and they enter thus. The first belongs to Salvatinica, and they come in one after the other. Some of the cars appear covered with many rich cloths, having on them many devices of dancing-girls and other human figures; there are other cars having tiers one on top of another, and others all of one kind; and so in their order they pass to where the king is. When the cars have gone out they are immediately followed by many horses covered with trappings and cloths of very fine stuff of the king's colours, and with many roses and flowers on their heads and necks, and with their bridles all gilded; and in front of these horses goes a horse with two state-umbrellas of the king, and with grander decorations than the others, and one of the lesser equerries leads it by the bridle. In front of this horse goes another caracoling and prancing, as do all horses here, being trained in that art. You must know that this horse that is conducted with all this state is a horse that the king keeps, on which they are sworn and received as kings, and on it must be sworn all those that shall come after them; and in case such a horse dies they put another in its place. If any king does not wish to be sworn on horseback, they swear him on an elephant, which they keep and treat with equal dignity.

These horses, then, going in the way I have stated, pass twice round the arena and place themselves in the middle of the arena in five or six lines, one before the other, and the king's horse in front of them, all facing the king; they stand in such a way that between them and the men there is an open space all round. As soon as they are arranged in this way and are all quiet there goes out from the inside of the palace a Brahman, the highest in rank of those about the king, and two others with him, and this chief Brahman carries in his hands a bowl with a cocoanut and some rice and flowers, while others carry a pot of water; and they pass round by the back of the horses, which all stand facing the king; and after performing his ceremonies there, he returns to the palace.

After this is over you will see issuing from inside twenty-five or thirty female doorkeepers, with canes in their hands and whips on their shoulders; and then close to these come many eunuchs, and after these eunuchs come many women playing many trumpets and drums and pipes (but not like ours) and viols, and many other kinds of music, and behind these women will come some twenty women-porters, with canes in their hands all covered with silver, and close to them come women clothed in the following manner. They have very rich and fine silk cloths; on the head they wear high caps which they call *collães*,[1] and on these caps they wear flowers made of large pearls; collars on the neck with jewels of gold very richly set with many emeralds and diamonds and rubies and pearls; and besides this many strings of pearls, and others for shoulder-belts; on the lower part of the arms many bracelets, with half of the upper arm all bare, having armlets in the same way all of precious stones; on the waist many girdles of gold and of precious stones, which girdles hang in order one below the other, almost as far down as half the thigh; besides these belts they have other jewels, and many strings of pearls round the ankles, for they wear very rich anklets even of greater value than the rest. They carry in their hands vessels of gold each as large as a small cask of water; inside these are some loops made of pearls fastened with wax, and inside all this a lighted lamp. They come in regular order one before the other, in all perhaps sixty women fair and young, from sixteen to twenty years of age. Who is he that

[1] *Kullāyi* in Telugu. See pp. 210, 252, note 2, and p. 383. These women appear to have worn men's head-dresses.

S

could tell of the costliness and the value of what each of these women carries on her person? So great is the weight of the bracelets and gold and jewels carried by them that many of them cannot support them, and women accompany them assisting them by supporting their arms. In this manner and in this array they proceed three times round the horses, and at the end retire into the palace. These women are maids of honour to the queens, and so are the others that go with them; on each day of these nine days of the feast one of the queens sends, each on her own day, her ladies with the others. The officials, in honour of the feast, have the days divided between them in accordance with their custom as already arranged by the king; and these women come every day most richly attired, taking pleasure in shewing themselves in such things, and in making a display each one of what she possesses.

When these women retire the horses also go, and then come the elephants, and after making their salaam they too retire. As soon as they are gone the king retires by a small door which is at the end of the building. Then the Brahmans go and take an idol, and carry it to the House of Victory, where is the room of cloth that I have spoken of; and the king at once comes from within, and goes to where the idol is, and offers his prayers and performs his ceremonies. Then they bring there more buffaloes and sheep, and kill them in the same way as before, and then come the professional women to dance. As soon as the slaughter of the buffaloes and sheep is over the king retires, and goes to his supper; for he fasts all these nine days, and (each day) they eat nothing until all is finished, and their hour for food is midnight. The bayadères remain dancing before the idol a long time after all this is done.

In this way are celebrated these festivals of nine days; on the last day there are slaughtered two hundred and fifty buffaloes and four thousand five hundred sheep.

When these days of festival are past, the king holds a review of all his forces, and the review is thus arranged. The king commands to pitch his tent of Mecca velvet a full league from the city, at a place already fixed for that purpose; and in this tent they place the idol in honour of which all these festivals are celebrated. From this tent to the king's palace the captains range themselves with their troops and array, each one in his place according to his rank in the king's household. Thus the soldiers stand in line; but it does not appear to you to be only one line but in some places two or three, one behind the other. Where there was a lake it was surrounded with troops, and where the road was narrow they were drawn up on the plain; and so on the slope of the hills and eminences, in such a way that you could see neither plain nor hill that was not entirely covered with troops. Those on foot stood in front of those on horses, and the elephants behind the horses; in this array was each captain with his troops. The captains who had their stations inside the city, since the soldiers could not be drawn up on the flat roofs of the houses, put up scaffoldings across the mouths of the streets to hold the troops, in such a way that all were full, both outside and in.

Now I should like to describe to you how they were armed, and their decorations. The cavalry were mounted on horses fully caparisoned, and on their foreheads plates, some of silver but most of them gilded, with fringes of twisted silk of all colours, and reins of the same;[1] others had trappings of Mecca velvet, which is velvet of many colours with fringes and ornaments; others had them of other silks, such as satins and damask, and others of brocade from China and

[1] The reins were not of leather, but of silk twisted into ropes.

Persia.[1] Some of the men with the gilded plates had them set with many large precious stones, and on the borders lace-work of small stones. Some of these horses had on their foreheads heads of serpents and of other large animals of various kinds, made in such a strange manner that they were a sight to see for the perfection of their make. The horsemen were dressed in quilted tunics,[2] also of brocade and velvet and every kind of silk. These tunics are made of layers of very strong raw leáther, and furnished with other iron (plates) that make them strong; some have these plates gilded both inside and out, and some are made of silver. Their headpieces are in the manner of helmets with borders covering the neck, and each has its piece to protect the face; they are of the same fashion as the tunics. They wear on the neck gorgets (*cofos*) all gilded, others made of silk with plates of gold and silver, others of steel as bright as a mirror. At the waists they have swords and small battle-axes, and in their hands javelins with the shafts covered with gold and silver. All have their umbrellas of state made of

[1] I read the word in the MS. *Xismael*, and Mr. Lopes suggests that this stands for Sheik (*Xeque*) Ismâîl. If so, undoubtedly Persia is meant.

[2] *Laudeis*. This word, variously spelt, is constantly used. It appears to refer to the thick quilted tunics, strengthened by leather or metal pieces, which were so often worn in India in old days. They were in many cases richly ornamented, and formed a good defence against sword-cuts. The pillars of the elaborately ornamented *Kalyâna Mandapa* of the temple in the fort at Vellore in North Arcot, which was built during the Vijayanagar period, are carved with rearing horses, whose riders wear jerkins, apparently of leather, fastened with buttons and loops. It is possible that this was the body-clothing referred to by the chronicler. I can give no clue to the origin of the word, unless it be connected with the Kanarese *lôdu*, "a stuffed cloth or cushion." Barros, describing the dress of the Hindu cavalry in the Raichûr campaign of 1520, says that they wore *laudees* of cotton (*embutidos*, whatever that may mean in this context—lit. "inlaid"), on body, head, and arms, strong enough to protect them against lance-thrusts or sword-cuts; the horses and elephants were similarly protected. Foot-soldiers carried no defensive armour "but only the *laudees*." —Dec. III. l. iv. c. 4.

embroidered velvet and damask, with many coloured silks on the horses. They wave many (standards with) white and coloured tails, and hold them in much esteem —which tails are horses' tails. The elephants in the same way are covered with caparison of velvet and gold with fringes, and rich cloths of many colours, and with bells so that the earth resounds; and on their heads are painted faces of giants and other kinds of great beasts. On the back of each one of them are three or four men, dressed in their quilted tunics, and armed with shields and javelins, and they are arrayed as if for a foray. Then, turning to the troops on foot, there are so many that they surround all the valleys and hills in a way with which nothing in the world can compare. You will see amongst them dresses of such rich cloths that I do not know where they came from, nor could any one tell how many colours they have; shield-men with their shields, with many flowers of gold and silver on them, others with figures of tigers and other great beasts, others all covered with silver leaf-work beautifully wrought, others with painted colours, others black and (so polished that) you can see into them as into a mirror, and their swords so richly ornamented that they could not possibly be more so. Of the archers, I must tell you that they have bows plated with gold and silver, and others have them polished, and their arrows very neat, and so feathered that they could not be better; daggers at their waists and battle-axes, with the shafts and ends of gold and silver; then you see musqueteers with their musquets and blunderbusses and their thick tunics, all in their order, with their . . .[1] in all their bravery; it was indeed a thing to see. Then the Moors —one must not forget them—for they were there also in the review with their shields, javelins, and Turkish bows, with many bombs and spears and fire-missiles;

[1] *Liões.* The meaning is not clear.

and I was much astonished to find amongst them men who knew so well how to work these weapons.

The king leaves his palace riding on the horse of which I have already told you, clothed in the many rich white cloths I have mentioned, with two umbrellas of state all gilded and covered with crimson velvet, and with the jewels and adornments which they keep for the purpose of wearing at such times: he who ever wears such jewels can understand the sort of things so great a lord would wear. Then to see the grandeur of the nobles and men of rank, I cannot possibly describe it all, nor should I be believed if I tried to do so; then to see the horses and the armour that they wear, you would see them so covered with metal plates that I have no words to express what I saw, and some hid from me the sight of others; and to try and tell of all I saw is hopeless, for I went along with my head so often turned from one side to the other that I was almost falling backwards off my horse with my senses lost. The cost of it all is not so much to be wondered at, as there is so much money in the land, and the chiefs are so wealthy.

There went in front of the king many elephants with their coverings and ornaments, as I have said; the king had before him some twenty horses fully caparisoned and saddled, with embroideries of gold and precious stones, that showed off well the grandeur and state of their lord. Close to the king went a cage such as is seen at Lisbon on the day of the Corpo de Dios festival, and it was gilded and very large; it seemed to me to be made of copper or silver; it was carried by sixteen men, eight on each side, besides others who took their turns, and in it is carried the idol of which I have already spoken. Thus accompanied the king passed along gazing at his soldiers, who gave great shouts and cries and struck their shields;

the horses neighed, the elephants screamed, so that it seemed as if the city would be overturned, the hills and valleys and all the ground trembled with the discharges of arms and musquets; and to see the bombs and fire-missiles over the plains, this was indeed wonderful. Truly it seemed as if the whole world were collected there.

In this way it went on till the king arrived at the place where the tent was that I have already mentioned, and he entered this and performed his usual ceremonies and prayers. You must not think that when the king passed the troops moved from their positions, on the contrary they stood motionless in their places till the king returned. As soon as the king had finished his ceremonies he again took horse and returned to the city in the same way as he had come, the troops never wearying of their shouting; as soon as he passed by them they began to march. Then to see those who were on the hills and slopes, and the descent of them with their shouts and beating of shields and shaking of arrows and bows that were without count. Truly, I was so carried out with myself that it seemed as if what I saw was a vision, and that I was in a dream. Then the troops began to march to their tents and pavilions in the plains, which were in great number; and all the captains accompanied the king as far as the palace, and thence departed to rest themselves from their labour.

Now I desire you to know that this king has continually a million fighting troops,[1] in which are included 35,000 cavalry in armour; all these are in his pay, and he has these troops always together and ready to be despatched to any quarter whenever such may be necessary. I saw, being in this city of Bisnaga, the king despatch a force against a place, one of those which

[1] As to this large number see p. 147 ff. above.

he has by the sea-coast; and he sent fifty captains with 150,000 soldiers, amongst whom were many cavalry. He has many elephants, and when the king wishes to show the strength of his power to any of his adversaries amongst the three kings bordering on his kingdom, they say that he puts into the field two million soldiers; in consequence of which he is the most feared king of any in these parts. And although he takes away so many men from his kingdom, it must not be thought that the kingdom remains devoid of men; it is so full that it would seem to you as if he had never taken away a man, and this by reason of the many and great merchants that are in it. There are working people and all other kinds of men who are employed in business, besides those who are obliged to go into the field; there are also a great number of Brahmans. In all the land of the heathen there are these Brahmans; they are men who do not eat anything that suffers death; they have little stomach for the use of arms.

Should any one ask what revenues this king possesses, and what his treasure is that enables him to pay so many troops, since he has so many and such great lords in his kingdom, who, the greater part of them, have themselves revenues, I answer thus: These captains whom he has over these troops of his are the nobles of his kingdom; they are lords, and they hold the city, and the towns and villages of the kingdom; there are captains amongst them who have a revenue of a million and a million a half of *pardaos*, others a hundred thousand *pardaos*, others two hundred, three hundred or five hundred thousand *pardaos*, and as each one has revenue so the king fixes for him the number of troops he must maintain, in foot, horse, and elephants.[1] These troops are always ready for duty,

[1] Some details are given by Nuniz (below, p. 384 f.).

THE ELEPHANT STABLES AT VIJAYANAGAR

From a Photograph by Col. W. Hooper)

whenever they may be called out and wherever they may have to go; and in this way he has this million of fighting men always ready. Each of these captains labours to turn out the best troops he can get because he pays them their salaries; and in this review there were the finest young men possible to be seen or that ever could be seen, for in all this array I did not see a man that would act the coward. Besides maintaining these troops, each captain has to make his annual payments to the king, and the king has his own salaried troops to whom he gives pay. He has eight hundred elephants attached to his person, and five hundred horses always in his stables, and for the expenses of these horses and elephants he has devoted the revenues that he receives from this city of Bisnaga. You may well imagine how great these expenses may be, and besides these that of the servants who have the care of the horses and elephants; and by this you will be able to judge what will be the revenue of this city.

This king of Bisnaga has five kings his subjects and vassals,[1] besides other captains and lords having large territories and great revenues; whenever a son happens to be born to this king, or a daughter, all the nobles of the kingdom offer him great presents of money and jewels of price, and so they do to him every year on the day of his birth.

You must know that when these feasts of which I have spoken are ended, at the beginning of the month of October, when eleven of its days are past, they make great feasts, during which every one puts on new, and rich, and handsome cloths, each one according to his liking, and all the captains give their

[1] According to the quite independent testimony of Nuniz (below, p. 374) these were the "kings" of Bankâpur, Gersoppa, Bakanûr Calicut, and Bhatkal.

men handsome cloths of many colours, each one having his own colour and device. On the same day they give great gifts of money to the king, it is even said that they give on that day to the king in money a million and five hundred thousand gold *pardaos*, and each *pardao* is worth three hundred and sixty *reis*, and from this you will be able to know how many *reis* there will be. I wish you to know that on this day begins their year; it is their New Year's Day, and for this they make the feast and give the gifts; and it is not to be wondered at, for we also do the same on New Year's Day. They begin the year in this month with the new moon, and they count the months always from moon to moon.[1]

And now I wish you to know that the previous kings of this place for many years past have held it a custom to maintain a treasury, which treasury, after the death of each, is kept locked and sealed in such a way that it cannot be seen by any one, nor opened, nor do the kings who succeed to the kingdom open them or know what is in them. They are not opened except when the kings have great need, and thus the kingdom has great supplies to meet its needs. This king has made his treasury different from those of the previous kings, and he puts in it every year ten million *pardaos*, without taking from them one *pardao* more than for the expenses of his house. The rest remains for him, over and above these expenses and of the expenses in the houses of his wives, of whom I have already told you that he keeps near him twelve thousand women; from this you will be able to judge how great is the richness of this kingdom, and how great the treasure that this king has amassed.

And if any one does not know what a *pardao* is,

[1] For a full note as to these chronological details see above, p. 140 ff.

let him know that it is a round gold coin, which coin is not struck anywhere in India except in this kingdom; it bears impressed on it on one side two images and on the other the name of the king who commanded it to be struck; those which this king ordered to be struck have only one image. This coin is current all over India. Each *pardao*, as already said, is worth three hundred and sixty *reis*.

After all these things (feasts) had passed the king betook himself to the new city, of which I have already told you that he delights in it much because it was made and peopled by him, of which I have already told you. In two years the king built this city. The king was received by the citizens with great feasts, and the streets were hung with rich cloths, and with many triumphal arches under which he passed. In this city the king held another review of the troops of his guard, and he distributed pay to all because it was the beginning of the year, and it is their custom to pay salaries year by year. An inspection is held by the officers of his house, and they write down the name of each one, and the marks that he has on his face or body. There are men of the guard who have a thousand *pardaos* pay, and others eight hundred, others six hundred and more, and a little more or less; there is a difference, and also a difference in the persons. Some men of them who are of higher rank than others have two horses or three, and others have no more than one. These troops have their captains, and each captain goes with his guard to mount guard at the palace according to order and custom; the king has in his guard five hundred horse, and these watch outside the palace armed with their weapons. There are two watches inside, and people with swords and shields.

The king, then, being in his new city, as I have said, Christovão de Figueiredo begged him of his kindness that he would permit him to be shown the palace of the city of Bisnaga, forasmuch as there had come with him many Portuguese who had never been in Bisnaga, and they would rejoice to see it, in order to have somewhat to tell of on their return to their own lands, whenever God should take them there. The king at once commanded that they should be shown certain of his residences, for that of his wives no one ever sees. As soon as we had returned to the city of Bisnaga, the governor of that place, who is called Gamdarajo, and is brother of Salvatinica,[1] showed us the palace.

You must know that on entering that gate of which I have spoken, by which the ladies serving the king's wives make their exit when they come to the feast, opposite to it there is another of the same kind. Here they bade us stand still, and they counted us how many we were, and as they counted they admitted us one by one to a small courtyard with a smoothly plastered floor, and with very white walls around it.[2] At the end of this courtyard, opposite this gate by which we entered, is another close to it on the left hand, and another which was closed; the door opposite belongs to the king's residence. At the entrance of this door outside are two images painted like life and drawn in their manner, which are these; the one on the right hand

[1] The "Guandaja" of Nuniz (below, p. 361).

[2] All these buildings are utterly destroyed, but there is no doubt that careful and systematic excavations would disclose the whole plan of the palace, and that in the ruins and débris would be found the remains of the beautiful sculptures described. Close behind the great decorated pavilion, from which the king and his court witnessed the feasts described by Paes, and therefore close to the gate just alluded to, are to be seen, half-buried in earth and débris, two large stone doors, each made of a single slab. The stone has been cut in panels to imitate woodwork, and has large staples carved from the same block.

is of the father of this king, and the one on the left is of this king. The father was dark and a gentleman of fine form, stouter than the son is; they stand with all their apparel and such raiment as they wear or used to wear when alive. Afterwards, wishing to pass in at this door, they again counted us, and after they had finished counting us we entered a little house which contained what I shall now relate.

As soon as you are inside, on the left hand, are two chambers one above the other, which are in this manner: the lower one is below the level of the ground, with two little steps which are covered with copper gilded, and from there to the top is all lined with gold (I do not say "gilded," but "lined" inside), and outside it is dome-shaped. It has a four-sided porch made of cane-work[1] over which is a work of rubies and diamonds and all other kinds of precious stones, and pearls, and above the porch are two pendants of gold; all the precious stone-work is in heart-shapes, and, interweaved between one and another, is a twist of thick seed-pearl work; on the dome are pendants of the same. In this chamber was a bed which had feet similar to the porch, the cross-bars covered with gold, and there was on it a mattress of black satin; it had all round it a railing of pearls a span wide; on it were two cushions and no other covering. Of the chamber above it I shall not say if it held anything because I did not see it, but only the one below on the right side. In this house there is a room with pillars of carved stone; this room is all of ivory, as well the chamber as the walls, from top to bottom, and the pillars of the cross-timbers at the top had roses and flowers of lotuses all of ivory, and all well executed, so that there

[1] *Feyto de huas meyas canas.* I am doubtful as to the meaning of this. Examination of the mass of ruins now remaining would settle all these points. Stone sculptures were broken up and left. They were not removed. (See also p. 288 below.)

could not be better,—it is so rich and beautiful that you would hardly find anywhere another such. On this same side is designed in painting all the ways of life of the men who have been here even down to the Portuguese, from which the king's wives can understand the manner in which each one lives in his own country, even to the blind and the beggars. In this house are two thrones covered with gold, and a cot of silver with its curtains. Here I saw a little slab of green jasper, which is held for a great thing in this house. Close to where this jasper is, *i.e.* underneath some arches where is the entrance into the palace, there is a little door closed with some padlocks: they told us that inside it there was a treasury of one of the former kings.

As soon as we left this house we entered a courtyard as large as an arena for beast-fights, very well plastered, and almost in the middle are some pillars of wood, with a cross beam at the top all covered with copper gilt, and in the middle four chains of silver links with hooks which are caught one into the other; this serves for a swing for the wives of the king. At the entrance of this courtyard on the right hand we mounted four or five steps and entered some beautiful houses made in the way I have already told you—for their houses are single-storeyed houses with flat roofs on top, although on top there may be other houses; the plan is good, and they are like terraces. There is a building there built on many pillars, which are of stone-work, and so also is all the work of the roof, with all the rest of wood (*maneria*), and all the pillars (with all the other work) are gilded so that they seem as if covered with gold.

Then at the entrance of this building in the middle nave, there is, standing on four pillars, a canopy covered with many figures of dancing-women, besides other small figures[1] which are placed in the stone-work. All this is also gilded, and has some red colour on the under-sides of the leaves which stand out from the sculpture. You must know that they make no use of this building because it belongs to their idol and to the temple. At the end of this is a little closed door where the idol is. Whenever they celebrate any festival of this idol, they carry it on a golden throne and put it underneath that canopy which is made for that purpose; and then come the Brahmans to perform their ceremonies there, and the dancing-girls come to dance.

Descending from this building, we passed on the left side of the courtyard, and we entered a corridor which runs the whole length of it, in which we saw some things. On entering the corridor was a cot suspended in the air by silver chains; the cot had feet made of bars of gold, so well made that they could not be better, and the cross-bars of the cot were covered with gold. In front of this cot was a chamber where was another cot suspended in the air by chains of gold; this cot had feet of gold with much setting of precious stones, and the cross-bars were covered with gold. Above this chamber was another, smaller, and with nothing in it save only that it was gilt and painted. Passing this chamber, along the same corridor in front was a chamber which this king commanded to be made; on the outside were figures of women with bows and arrows like amazons. They had begun to paint this chamber, and they told us that it had to be finer than the others, and that it was to be all plated with gold, as well the ground below as all the rest. Passing this corridor and mounting up into another which is higher, we saw at one end three caldrons of gold, so large that in each one they could

[1] Mr. Ferguson has ingeniously emendated Senhor Lopes's reading, from *yinagees por que nas que estão metidas* to *ymagees pequenas que*, &c. . . . The MS., however, which is itself a copy, has *por que nas*.

cook half a cow, and with them were others, very large ones, of silver, and also little pots of gold and some large ones. Thence we went up by a little staircase, and entered by a little door into a building which is in this manner. This hall is where the king sends his women to be taught to dance. It is a long hall and not very wide, all of stone sculpture on pillars, which are at a distance of quite an arm's length from the wall; between one and another is an arm's length and a half, perhaps a little more. These pillars stand in that manner all around the building; they are half-pillars (?)[1] made with other hollows (?) all gilt.[2] In the supports (or pedestals) on the top[3] are many great beasts like elephants, and of other shapes; it is open so that the interior is seen, and there are on the inner side of these beasts other images, each placed according to its character; there are also figures of men turned back to back, and other beasts of different sorts. In each case from pillar to pillar is a cross-bar (the architrave) which is like a panel, and from pillar to pillar are many such panels; there are images of old men, too, gilded and of the size of a cubit. Each of the panels has one placed in this way. These images are over all the building. And on the pillars are other images, smaller, with other images yet more subordinate, and other figures again, in such a way that I saw this work gradually diminishing in size on these pillars with their designs, from pillar to pillar,

[1] *São de meas canas* (see above, p. 285). Meaning not understood, unless it be as rendered.

[2] This description deserves special notice. The writer is evidently describing a *mandapa* richly sculptured, of which so many examples are still to be seen in temples, and he states that the whole of the stone carving was richly coloured and gilded. This probably was always the case. Traces of colour still remain on many of these buildings at Vijayanagar.

[3] *Pranhus* (see above, p. 241). Probably the sculptures were like many still to be seen in the temples of that date in Southern India, where the base of the pillar is elaborately carved with grotesque figures of elephants, horses, and monsters.

and each time smaller by the size of a span as it went on, becoming lost; so it went dwindling gradually away till there remained of all the sculptured work only the dome, the most beautiful I ever saw. Between these images and pillars runs a design of foliage, like plates (*a maneyra de lamines*), all gilt, with the reverses of the leaves in red and blue, the images that are on the pillars are stags and other animals, they are painted in colours with the pink on their faces; but the other images seated on the elephants, as well as those on the panels, are all dancing women having little drums (tom-toms).

The designs of these panels show the positions at the ends of dances in such a way that on each panel there is a dancer in the proper position at the end of the dance; this is to teach the women, so that if they forget the position in which they have to remain when the dance is done, they may look at one of the panels where is the end of that dance. By that they keep in mind what they have to do.

At the end of this house on the left hand is a painted recess where the women cling on with their hands in order better to stretch and loosen their bodies and legs; there they teach them to make the whole body supple, in order to make their dancing more graceful. At the other end, on the right, in the place where the king places himself to watch them dancing, all the floors and walls where he sits are covered with gold, and in the middle of the wall is a golden image of a woman of the size of a girl of twelve years, with her arms in the position which she occupies in the end of a dance.

They did not show us more than this. The residence of the women no one may see except the eunuchs, of whom I have already told you. From here we returned by the way we had entered to the second gate, and there they again counted us.

T

Of the city of Bisnaga they say that there are more than a hundred thousand dwelling-houses in it, all one-storeyed and flat-roofed, to each of which there is a low surrounding wall, and in this city the king lives most of the time. On the north side are rocky hills; a river runs between them, and the wall runs along the top of them, and on the farther side is a city called Nagumdym; and it has only three gates, namely one by the river, which they cross in boats embarking just at this gate;[1] one on the other side which is to the north, this is a stronger gate; and one on the north-west side, a little gate between two very high ridges; and it is such a bad road that only one horseman can pass out a time.

And on the north-west side (of Bisnaga) is another city called Crisnapor[2] connected with Bisnaga, in which are all their pagodas, those in which they most worship, and all the revenue of this city is granted to them; and they say that they have a revenue of a hundred thousand *pardaos* of gold. The pagodas are high and have great buildings with many figures of men and women, all in lascivious attitudes.

On the south side is the other city called Nagalapor in a plain; in it the Ydalcão stopped with all his forces when he besieged Bisnaga, and he razed it to the ground; but already it is again rebuilt, and this is a league from Bisnaga.[3]

On the east side is another city called Ardegema,[4] which is the name of the principal wife of this king, and it is new, and he built it for love of her.

[1] The gate still exists opposite the Ânegundi ferry.

[2] Krishnâpura, where are the ruins of a fine temple.

[3] It seems clear that this sentence must be interpolated, and perhaps also the whole of the last four paragraphs. For the penultimate sentence could not have formed part of the original chronicle of Paes, written perhaps in 1522, or thereabouts, as it refers to an event that took place in 1535–36.

[4] Elsewhere called "Ondegema." Its other name was Nâgalâpur. It is the modern Hospett. (See below, Nuniz, p. 387.)

CHRONICLE OF FERNÃO NUNIZ

(WRITTEN, PROBABLY, A.D. 1535–37)

CHAPTER I

Copy and Summary of a Chronicle of the Kings of Bisnaga, who reigned (orig. were) from the era one thousand two hundred and thirty, which was after the general destruction of the kingdom of Bisnaga.[1]

IN the year twelve hundred and thirty[2] these parts of India were ruled by a greater monarch than had ever reigned. This was the King of Dili,[3] who by force of arms and soldiers made war on Cambaya for many years, taking and destroying in that period the land of Guzarate which belongs to Cambaya,[4] and in the end he became its lord.

And this taken, not being content with the victory which he had already gained, he made ready a large army of foot and horse, and determined to make war on the King of Bisnaga, leaving his captains in his lands and fortresses to defend themselves against his enemies, of whom there were many; for this King[5] was at that time at war with Bemgalla, and with the Turkomans on the confines of the country of Sheikh Ismael.[6] These men are fair and large of body; in their lands are

[1] This "general destruction" evidently refers to the conquest of Ânegundi by Muhammad Taghlaq.

[2] (See above, p. 8.) The date should be about 1330. Nuniz was here about a century wrong.

[3] Delhi.

[4] A common error with the foreigners. Properly speaking it was Cambaya which belonged to Gujarât.

[5] Muhammad Taghlaq of Delhi.

[6] Persia (above, p. 10).

many horses with which this King of Delly made war on Cambaya and laid it waste; and after the country was taken and he lord of it, there still remained to him as many as eight hundred thousand horsemen with whom he passed on to Bisnaga; of the number of people on foot nothing is said here because no one counted them.

And, determining to make war on the King of Bisnaga and to reduce him under his rule, he passed out of the lands which he had newly gained, entering into those of the King of Bisnaga, which at that time were many; and quitting the kingdom of Cambaya, he began to invade and make war on the Ballagate,[1] whose lands now belong to the Idalcão,[2] taking and destroying many towns and places in such a way that the people of the country surrendered to him their persons and property, though he left to them their weapons which he could not prevent their carrying.

And after he had become lord of all the country of the Ballagate, he passed the river of Duree,[3] which forms the boundary of the territories of the Ballagate and of those of the King of Bisnaga, which river he passed in basket-boats without finding any one to oppose the passage. Up to that time, in all that was (afterwards) the kingdom of Bisnaga, no place was populated save only the city of Nagumdym,[4] in which the King of Bisnaga[5] then was, awaiting his

[1] *i.e.* the Bâlâghât, or country above the ghâts. "The high land on the top is very flatte and good to build upon, called Ballagatte and Decan, and is inhabited and divided among divers kings and governors" (Linschoten, i. 65). Correa divides this part of India into "Bisnega, Balagate, and Cambay."

[2] This is the Portuguese rendering of the Âdil Khân, or Âdil Shâh of Bîjapûr. "Idalxa" represents the latter title.

[3] The description applies best to the Mâlprabha River, and perhaps "Duree" represents Dhârwâr.

[4] Ânegundi.

[5] He was at that time only chief or king of Ânegundi, Vijayanagar not having been yet founded.

destruction, since it was strong, and because he possessed no other citadel but that, which was his Lisbon.

And from the river which that King of Delly passed in basket-boats,[1] to that city was twenty-five leagues, all being open country (*campos*); and in them it seemed good to him to pitch his camp, so that his people might drink of the water in the plain (*campos*) along the length of the river. At that time there was great drought by reason of the summer season, and the waters of the few little lakes that were in the plain would not suffice for ten days for his troops, horses, and elephants, without drying up; and for that reason he halted some days by the banks of that river, till rain fell in the fields and lakes, enough for such a large army as he had brought with him.

And when the time came he raised his camp and brought his array to a halt in sight of that city of Nagundy.

And the King of Bisnaga, seeing his great power and how many troops he had brought with him, determined to abandon the city, which was very difficult to enter; close to which was, and now is, a river which is called Nagundy, whence the city is called Nagundy, and they say the city had its name because of it. And he fled for shelter to a fortress called Crynamata,[2] which was by the bank of the river, and which contained much provision and water; but not enough for the sustenance of so many people as he had with him, as many as fifty thousand men. Therefore the King chose five thousand men with their property and took refuge in the fortress; and for the

[1] These basket-boats are described by Paes (see above, p. 259).

[2] I have not been able to identify this name. It is possible that the first syllable represents the word *Srî*, and that the whole may have been a special appellation of the upper fortress or citadel, on the rocky heights above the town of Ânegundi.

rest he bade them betake themselves to another fortress of his in another part of his kingdom.

And being sheltered in the fortress, after he had taken order about his provisions, he was beset on all sides by the King of the people of Dely, who had already up to this time been at war with him[1] for twelve years; over which siege little time was spent, because the people that were inside the fortress were numerous, and in a little space had consumed their provisions.

Then the King of Bisnaga, seeing the determination of the soldiers of the King of Delly that they would never leave the place without making an end of those whom he had with him in the fortress, made a speech to them all, laying before them the destruction that the King of the troops of Dely had caused in his own kingdoms;[2] and how, not content with that, he had besieged this fortress, so that now there was nothing for them to look to but death, since already there was no water in the fortress nor anything left to eat. And (he said) that of the fifty thousand men who had been in the city of Nagundy he had chosen them alone as his companions and true friends, and he begged of them that they would hold fast in death to the loyalty which they had borne him in their lives; for he hoped that day to give battle to the King of Delly. Then he said that already there remained to him of his kingdom and lordship nothing but that fortress and the people that were in it, and so he asked them to arm themselves and die with him in battle, giving their lives to the enemy who had deprived them of all their lands.

[1] There had been no special war with Ânegundi that we know of; but the Râjah of that place had very possibly been directly affected by, if not actually engaged in, the wars between the Hindu Hoysala Ballâlas and the rulers of Warangal and Gujarât on the one hand, and the Muhammadan invaders from Delhi on the other.

[2] See Introduction, p. 13. "His kingdoms" (*seus reynos*) refers to the territories of Muhammad Taghlaq, whose barbarities had resulted in the wasting and depopulation of large tracts.

All of them were very content and glad at this, and in a short space were all armed; and after they were so the King made them another speech, saying, "Before we join battle we have to wage another war with our sons and daughters and wives, for it will not be good that we should allow them to be taken for the use of our enemies." And the King said, "I will be the first to deal with my wife and sons." At this time they were all standing in a large open space which was before the citadel, and there by the hand of the King were slain over fifty of his wives and some sons and little daughters; and the same was done with their own hands by all who had wives and sons that could not fight.

When these nuptial feasts, so abhorred of all, were fulfilled, they opened the gates of the fortress, and their enemies forthwith entered, and slew all of them except six old men who withdrew to a house. These were made captive and were taken before the King (of Delhi), and the King asked them who they were and how they had escaped, and they told them who they were; at which the King greatly rejoiced, because one of them was the minister of the kingdom and another the treasurer, and the others were leading officers in it. They were questioned by the King concerning the treasures of the King of Bisnaga, and such riches as were buried in the vaults of the fortress were delivered up to him; they also gave him an account of the revenues of the kingdom of Bisnaga at that time. When all was known to the King he delivered them to one of his captains, and commanded to make over the bodies of the dead to another captain, and gave orders that the bodies should be burned; and the body of the King, at the request of those six men, was conveyed very honourably to the city of Nagundy. From that time forward that place became a burying-place of the kings. Amongst themselves they still worship this King as a saint.

CHAPTER II

Of what the King (of Delhi) did after he had slain the King of Bisnaga, and entirely overthrown him, and seized his lands for himself, none being left to defend them.

As soon as the King had thus fulfilled all his desires, he bade his captains destroy some villages and towns which had risen against him, and give security to those who sought it of him. After the death of the (Hindu) King he stayed in that fortress two years, having already for twelve waged war on the kingdom.[1] He was far from his home, which was more than five hundred leagues distant; and, his forces being all scattered, news came to him how that all the land which was first gained by him had rebelled. As soon as this was known to the King he sent to collect his people, leaving in this fortress, which was the strongest in the kingdom, abundant provisions for its defence in all circumstances; and he left, for captain and governor of the kingdom, Enybiquymelly,[2] a Moor, and with him he left many troops, showing much kindness to each one of them separately, giving to each lavish gifts and lands in such a way that all were content, and, abandoning forthwith all hope of returning to their own country, made there their homes.

CHAPTER III

How the King of Dily departed with his troops, and took to his kingdom the six captives that he had taken in the fortress, &c.

THE King having departed to his own kingdom in consequence of the news that had been brought to him, leaving the kingdom of Bisnaga in the power of Meli-

[1] See above, p. 294, note 1.

[2] Spelt below "Meliquy niby" and "Mileque neby;" evidently for *Mallik Naib*, the king's deputy.

quy niby, when it was known throughout the country how he was out of it, those who had escaped to the mountains, with others who, against their will and through fear had taken oaths of fealty for their towns and villages, rose against the captain Mileque neby, and came to besiege him in the fortress, allowing no provisions to go in to him, nor paying him the taxes that had been forced on them. And Meliquy niby, seeing how little profit he could get in this country, and how badly he was obeyed, and how far off was the succour sent by his lord the King, sent quickly to him to tell him how all the land was risen against him, and how every one was lord of what he pleased, and no one was on his side; and that His Highness should decide what he thought best to be done in such case. And when the King heard this news he took counsel, telling the great people of the realm of the letter and message which he had from Melinebiquy, his captain and governor of the kingdom of Bisnaga, and how badly the lords of the land obeyed him; so that each one was king and lord over whomsoever he pleased, as soon as he acquired any power, there being no justice amongst them, nor any one whom they wished to obey. What was it seemed best to them (he asked), and what in such case ought they, and could they, do, so that he should not lose so fair a territory and one so rich, the seizure of which had cost such labour, so much money, and the lives of so many of their fellows? All the councillors decided that the King should command the presence of the six men whom he held captive, and that he should learn from them who was at that time the nearest of kin, or in any way related to the Kings of Bisnaga; and, this questioning done, no one was found to whom by right the kingdom could come, save to one of the six whom he held captive, and this one he who at the time of the destruction of Bisnaga had been minister of the kingdom. He was not related by blood to the kings, but only was the principal judge; but (it seemed) good that His Highness should give the kingdom to that one. And this advice pleased the King and them all.

At once the six captives were released and set at liberty, and many kindnesses and honours were done them, and the governor was raised to be King and the treasurer to be governor;[1] and he took from them oaths and pledges of their fealty as vassals; and they were at once despatched and sent to their lands with a large following to defend them from any one who should desire to do them an injury. And when these six men had thus finished their journey to the city of Nagundy, they found only the ruined basements of the houses, and places peopled by a few poor folk.

In a short time the arrival of Deoráo[2] (for so he was called) was known in all the country, and how he had been exalted to be King, with which the people were well content, as men who had felt so deeply their subjection to a lord not of their own faith; and from this man have descended all those who have reigned up to now. And they made great feasts for him, and delivered up to him the lands taken by former kings and lost to them, and he was obeyed as King. And when the captain Meliquy niby became aware of this, he was very pleased and contented, and delivered up to him the fortress and kingdom as the King his lord had commanded; and making himself ready with all speed he departed, leaving the land to its proper owner. And after he had gone, King Deoráo, entering on his rule, strove to pacify the people and those who had

[1] Above, p. 19 ff.

[2] Deva Râya. This was the general title of the Vijayanagar kings; thus, Harihara Deva Râya, Bukka Deva Râya, Krishna Deva Râya, &c. This first king is given no personal name by Nuniz. There were afterwards two kings who are known to history by the names Deva Râya I. and Deva Râya II., with no personal name prefixed.

revolted, and to make them safe, and he did them many kindnesses so as to secure their good-will, and travelled about their fortresses and towns. He abandoned the lost lands since he knew that he could not regain them, having no army or forces for such a work, nor any cause for which he could make war; and also because he was very old.

CHAPTER IV

How the City of Bisnaga was built by that King Dehorão.

THE King going one day a-hunting, as was often his wont, to a mountain on the other side of the river of Nagumdym, where now is the city of Bisnaga,—which at that time was a desert place in which much hunting took place, and which the King had reserved for his own amusement,—being in it with his dogs and appurtenances of the chase, a hare rose up before him, which, instead of fleeing from the dogs, ran towards them and bit them all, so that none of them dared go near it for the harm that it did them.[1] And seeing this, the King, astonished at so feeble a thing biting dogs which had already caught for him a tiger and a lion, judged it to be not really a hare but (more likely) some prodigy; and he at once turned back to the city of Nagumdym.

And arriving at the river, he met a hermit who was walking along the bank, a man holy among them, to whom he told what had happened concerning the hare. And the hermit, wondering at it, said to the King that he should turn back with him and shew him the place where so marvellous a thing had happened; and being

[1] This same tale is told of many kings and chiefs in Southern India. The "Tazkarat-ul-Mulûk" (*Ind. Ant.*, May 1899, p. 129) also relates it of the Bahmanî Sultan Ahmad Shah (1422–35), alleging that it was the behaviour of a hunted hare that induced him to make Bîdar his capital.

there, the hermit said that the King ought in that place to erect houses in which he could dwell, and build a city, for the prodigy meant that this would be the strongest city in the world, and that it would never be captured by his enemies, and would be the chief city in the kingdom. And so the King did, and on that very day began work on his houses, and he enclosed the city round about; and that done he left Nagumdym and soon filled the new city with people. And he gave it the name Vydiajuna, for so the hermit called himself[1] who had bidden him construct it; but in course of time this name has become corrupted, and it is now called Bisnaga. And after that hermit was dead the King raised a very grand temple[2] in honour of him and gave much revenue to it. And ever since, in his memory, the Kings of Bisnaga, on the day when they are raised to be kings, have, in honour of the hermit, to enter this house before they enter their own; and they offer many prayers in it, and celebrate many feasts there every year.

This King Dehoráo reigned seven years, and did nothing therein but pacify the kingdom, which he left in complete tranquillity.

By his death one called Bucaráo[3] inherited the kingdom, and he conquered many lands which at the time of the destruction of that kingdom remained rebellious, and by him they were taken and turned to his power and lordship; and he took the kingdom of Orya, which is very great; it touches on Bemgalla. He reigned thirty-seven years, being not less feared than esteemed, and obeyed by all in his kingdom.

On the death of that King Bucaráo there came to

[1] This was the great Sringêri Guru, Mâdhavâchârya, surnamed *Vidyâranya*, or "Forest of Learning." This derivation of the name of the city is very common, but is believed to be erroneous.

[2] The large temple of Virûpâksha at Hampe.

[3] Bukka Râya.

the throne his son called Pureoyre Deoráo,[1] which in Canara means "powerful lord," and he coined a money of *pardaos* which even now they call "*puroure deoráo*;" and from that time forward it has become a custom to call coins by the names of the kings that made them; and it is because of this that there are so many names of *pardaos* in the kingdom of Bisnaga. And this King in his time did nothing more than leave at his death as much conquered country as his father had done.

This King had a son who by his death inherited the kingdom, who was called Ajaráo;[2] and he reigned forty-three years, in which time he was always at war with the Moors; and he took Goa, and Chaul, and Dabull, and Ceillão,[3] and all the country of Charamamdell,[4] which had also rebelled after the first destruction of this kingdom, and he did many other things which are not recorded here.

This King made in the city of Bisnaga many walls and towers and enclosed it anew. Now the city at that time was of no use, there being no water in it by which could be raised gardens and orchards, except the water of the Nagumdym which was far from it, for what water there was in the country was all brackish and allowed nothing to grow; and the King, desiring to increase that city and make it the best in the kingdom, determined to bring to it a very large river which was at a distance of five leagues away, believing that it would cause much profit if brought inside the city. And so he did, damming the river itself with great boulders; and according to story he threw in a stone so great that it alone made the river follow the King's will. It was dragged thither

1 *Pureoyre* probably represents "Harihara." This king was not the first to coin *pardaos* or pagodas. A pagoda of Bukka I. is known (*Ind. Ant.*, xx. 302).

2 See above, p. 51. There is no name amongst those of this dynasty with which this can be at present connected.

3 Ceylon.

4 Coromandel (note, p. 239 above).

by a number of elephants of which there are many in the kingdom; and the water so brought he carried through such parts of the city as he pleased. This water proved of such use to the city that it increased his revenue by more than three hundred and fifty thousand *pardaos*. By means of this water they made round about the city a quantity of gardens and orchards and great groves of trees and vineyards, of which this country has many, and many plantations of lemons and oranges and roses, and other trees which in this country bear very good fruit. But on this turning of the river they say the King spent all the treasure that had come to him from the king his father, which was a very great sum of money.

This King left a son at his death called Visaráo,[1] who inherited the kingdom on the death of his father; and he lived six years, and during this time did nothing worth relating.

At his death he left a son called Deoráo, who reigned twenty-five years. He determined to collect great treasures, but owing to constant warfare he could not gain more than eight hundred and fifty millions of gold, not counting precious stones. This was no great sum, seeing that in his time the King of Coullão,[2] and Ceyllão, and Paleacate,[3] and Peguu, and Tanaçary[4] and many other countries, paid tribute to him.

At his death this King left a son who inherited the kingdom, who was called Pinaráo,[5] he reigned twelve years, and was a great astrologer; he was given much to letters, and made many books and (promulgated) ordinances in his land and kingdom. As long as he

[1] Vijaya Rao. [2] Quilon.

[3] Pulicat, near Madras. This was an important province of Vijayanagar in later years. [4] Tenasserim.

[5] *Pina*=*Chinna* in Telugu, *Chikka* in Kanarese, and means "little." Pina Râya or Chikka Râya was the title applied to the Crown Prince (above, p. 223). The derivation given by Nuniz is plainly wrong.

reigned he had twenty ministers, which is an office that amongst these (people) is (generally) held only by one person. This King was very wise; he was well versed in all his duties, and possessed such good talents and qualities that they called him Pinaráo, which amongst them, in the language of Canara, means a very wise man. This King was killed by treason by the hand of a nephew whom he had brought up in his house like a son, who thus caused the death of the King.[1] The nephew resolved to marry, and for the feasts at his wedding he prayed the King, his uncle, that he would command that he should be attended and honoured at his wedding by the King's own son; and the King, for the love that he bore him and the pleasure that he had in honouring him, bade his son make ready with his following, and sent him with the ministers and captains of his court to attend and honour the wedding of his nephew. And he, making all ready, as soon as they were in his house, being at table, they were all slain by daggers thrust by men kept in readiness for that deed. This was done without any one suspecting it, because the custom there is to place on the table all that there is to eat and drink, no man being present to serve those who are seated, nor being kept outside, but only those who are going to eat; and because of their thus being alone at table, nothing of what passed could be known to the people they had brought with them. And after he had killed the King's son with all the captains, the minister[2] set out to ride as if he were going to bear a present to the King, and as soon as he arrived at the gates of the palace he sent a message to the King saying that he was there, and had brought

[1] Abdur Razzák relates the same story, and fixes the event as having taken place between November 1442 and April 1443 A.D., "while he was at Calicut" (above, p. 73).

[2] This seems to imply that the nephew of the king had been one of the twenty ministers (*regedores*) mentioned in the chronicle.

him a present according to custom. And the King, being at that time at leisure and amusing himself with his wives, bade him enter; and as soon as he was come to where he stood, he presented to the King a golden bowl in which he had placed a dagger steeped in poison, with which he wounded him in many places; but the King, as he was a man who knew how to use both sword and dagger better than any one in his kingdom, avoided by twists and turns of his body the thrusts aimed at him, freed himself from him, and slew him with a short sword that he had. And this done he ordered a horse to be saddled, and mounted it, and rode holding his nephew's head in his hand; and he took the road to the latter's house, apprehending that treason might have been wrought and fearing that his son might be dead. And as soon as he arrived he beheld the treason in very deed, and how wicked a deed his nephew had done; seeing that his son and his principal captains were dead, and that the traitor might have prevailed against himself had he had the power. In great wrath the King commanded his men to inflict dreadful punishments on all found guilty of this treason, and indeed many who were not so. He himself remained grievously wounded with the poisoned wounds and he lasted only six months, and these ended, died of the poison carried on the dagger.

After his death a son remained to him who inherited the kingdom and was called . . . [1], and this King, as soon as he began to reign, sent to call his treasurers and the minister and the scribes of his household, and inquired of them the revenue of his kingdom, and learned how much revenue came in yearly; and His Highness had every year thirteen millions of gold. This King granted to the pagodas a fifth part of the revenue of his kingdom; no law is possible in the

[1] *Sic* in orig.

country where these pagodas are, save only the law of the Brahmans, which is that of the priests; and so the people suffer.

On the death of this King succeeded a son named Verupacarao.[1] As long as he reigned he was given over to vice, caring for nothing but women, and to fuddle himself with drink and amuse himself, and never showed himself either to his captains or to his people; so that in a short time he lost that which his forefathers had won and left to him. And the nobles of the kingdom, seeing the habits and life of this king, rebelled, every one of them, each holding to what he possessed, so that in his time the King lost Goa, and Chaull, and Dabull, and the other chief lands of the realm. This King in mere sottishness slew many of his captains. Because he dreamed one night that one of his captains entered his chamber, on the next day he had him called, telling him that he had dreamed that night that the captain had entered his room to kill him; and for that alone he had him put to death. This King had two sons already grown up, who, seeing the wickedness of their father and how he had lost his kingdom, determined to kill him, as in fact was done by one of them, the elder, who was his heir; and after he had killed him, when they besought him to be King, he said, "Although this kingdom may be mine by right, I do not want it because I killed my father, and did therein that which I ought not to have done, and have committed a mortal sin, and for that reason it is not well that such an unworthy son should inherit the kingdom. Take my brother and let him govern it since he did not stain his hands with his father's blood;" which was done, and the younger brother was raised to the throne. And when they had entrusted the kingdom to him he was advised by his minister and captains that he should slay

[1] Virûpâksha Râya.

U

his brother, because, as the latter had killed his father so he would kill him if desirous of so doing; and as it appeared to the King that such a thing might well be, he determined to kill him, and this was at once carried out, and he slew him with his own hand. So that this man truly met the end that those meet with who do such ill deeds. This King was called Padearáo; and after this was done he gave himself up to the habits of his father, and, abandoning himself to his women, and not seeking to know ought regarding his realm save only the vices in which he delighted, he remained for the most part in the city.

One of his captains who was called Narsymgua,[1] who was in some manner akin to him, seeing his mode of life, and knowing how ill it was for the kingdom that he should live and reign, though all was not yet lost, determined to attack him and seize on his lands; which scheme he at once put into force.

He wrote, therefore, and addressed the captains and chiefs of the kingdom, saying how bad it was for them not to have a King over them who could govern properly, and how it would be no wonder, seeing the manner of his life, if the King soon lost by his bad government even more than his father had done.

He made great presents to all of them so as to gain their goodwill, and when he had thus attached many people to himself he made ready to attack Bisnaga where the King dwelt. When the King was told of the uprising of this captain Narsymgua, how he was approaching and seizing his lands and how many people were joining him, he seemed unmindful of the loss he had suffered, he gave no heed to it nor made ready, but, instead, he only ill-treated him who had brought the

[1] *Narasimha.* He had apparently large tracts of country under his charge to the east of the capital towards the east coast. His relationship to the sovereign has always been a matter of doubt.

news. So that a captain of the army of this Narsymgua arrived at the gates of Bisnaga, and there was not a single man defending the place; and when the King was told of his arrival he only said that it could not be. Then the captain entered the city, and the King only said that it could not be. Then he even entered his palace and came as far as the doors of his chamber, slaying some of the women. At last the King believed, and seeing now how great was the danger, he resolved to flee by the gates on the other side; and so he left his city and palaces, and fled.

When it was known by the captain that the King had fled he did not trouble to go after him, but took possession of the city and of the treasures which he found there; and he sent to acquaint his lord, Narsymgua. And after that Narsymgua was raised to be king. And as he had much power and was beloved by the people, thenceforward this kingdom of Bisnaga was called the kingdom of Narsymga.

After he was raised to be king and was obeyed he came to Bisnaga, where he did many acts of justice; and he took the territories from whomsoever had, contrary to right, taken them from the king. This King reigned forty-four years, and at his death left all the kingdom in peace, and he regained all the lands which the kings his predecessors had lost. He caused horses to be brought from Oromuz and Adeem [1] into his kingdom and thereby gave great profit to the merchants, paying them for the horses just as they asked. He took them dead or alive at three for a thousand *pardaos*, and of those that died at sea they brought him the tail only, and he paid for it just as if it had been alive.

At the death of that King there remained three fortresses which had revolted from his rule, and which

[1] Persia (Ormuz) and Aden. The latter were Arabs.

he was never able to take, which were these—Rachol, and Odegary and Conadolgi,[1] which have large and rich territories and are the principal forts in the kingdom. At his death he left two sons, and the governor of the kingdom was Nasenaque, who was father of the king that afterwards was king of Bisnaga;[2] and this king (Narsymgua), before he died, sent to call Narsenaque his minister, and held converse with him, telling him that at his death he would by testament leave him to govern the kingdom until the princes should be of an age to rule; also he said that all the royal treasures were his alone, and he reminded him that he had won this kingdom of Narsymgua at the point of the sword; adding that now there remained only three fortresses to be taken, but that for him the time for their capture was passed; and the King begged him to keep good guard over the kingdom and to deliver it up to the princes, to whichever of them should prove himself most fitted for it. And after the King's death this Narsenaque remained as governor, and soon he raised up the prince to be king, retaining in his own hands the treasures and revenues and the government of the country.

At that time a captain who wished him ill, determined to kill the prince, with a view afterwards to say that Narsenaque had bidden him commit the murder, he being the minister to whom the government of the kingdom had been entrusted, and he thought that for this act of treason Narsenaque would be put to death. And he soon so arranged it that the prince was killed one night by one of his pages who had been bribed

[1] "Rachol" is Raichûr; "Odegary" represents Udayagiri; "Conadolgi" probably is Kondavîd, *dolgi* for *drûg*, a mountain fortress.

[2] This account of the second Narasa and the family relationship differs altogether from the results obtained from epigraphical study, according to which the second Narasa was elder son of the first Narasa or Narasimha Krishna Deva being the latter's younger son.

for that purpose, and who slew the prince with a sword. As soon as Narsenaque heard that he was dead, and learned that he himself (was supposed to have) sent to kill him, he raised up another brother of the late King's to be king, not being able further to punish this captain, because he had many relations, until after he had raised this younger brother to be king, who was called Tamarao. He (Narsenaque) went out one day from the city of Bisnaga towards Nagumdym, saying that he was going hunting, leaving all his household in the city. And after he had arrived at this city of Nagumdym he betook himself to another called Penagumdim,[1] which is four-and-twenty leagues from that place, where he at once made ready large forces and many horses and elephants, and then sent to tell the King Tamarao of the cause of his going; relating to him the treason that that captain by name Tymarsaa[2] had carried out slaying his brother the king, and by whose death he (the prince) had inherited the kingdom. He told him how that the kingdom had been entrusted to him by his father, as well as the care of himself and his brother, that as this man had killed his brother, so he would do to him in the same way, for he was a traitor; and he urged that for that reason it was necessary to punish him. But the king at that time was very fond of that captain, since by reason of him he had become King, and in place of punishing him he bestowed favour on him and took his part against the minister. And, seeing this, Narsenaque went against him with large forces, and besieged him, threatening him for four or five days, until the King, seeing his determination, commanded Timarsaa to be put to death; after which he (the King) sent the (traitor's) head to be shown to the minister, who greatly rejoiced. Narsenaque sent away all

[1] Pennakonda.

[2] *Cf.* "Temersea," p. 250, and note. This, however, was not the man there alluded to, though he bore the same name.

the troops and entered the city, where he was very well received by all the people, by whom he was much loved as being a man of much justice.

And after some days and years had passed, Narsenaque, seeing the age of the king how young he was, determined to keep him in the city of Penagumdy, with large guards to make safe his person, and to give him 20,000 cruzados of gold every year for his food and expenses, and himself to govern the kingdom—for it had been entrusted to him by the king his lord so to do. After this had been done he told the King that he desired to go to Bisnaga to do certain things that would tend to the benefit of the kingdom, and the King, pleased at that, told him that so it should be; thinking that now he himself would be more his own master and not be so liable to be checked by him. And after he had departed and arrived at Bisnaga, Narsenaque sent the King 20,000 men for his guard, as he had arranged, and he sent as their captain Timapanarque, a man in whom he much confided; (commanding him) that he should not allow the King to leave the city, and that he should carefully guard his person against treachery.

And after this was done Narsenaque began to make war on several places, taking them and demolishing them because they had revolted. At that time it was proposed by some captains that they should kill the King, as he was not a man fitted to govern, but to this Narsenaque would answer nothing. After some days had passed, however, Narsenaque, pondering on the treason about which they had spoken to him, how it would increase his greatness and more easily make him lord of the kingdom of which he was (only) minister, called one day those same captains who had often proposed it to him, and asked them by what means the King could be slain without its being known that he had had a hand in his death. Then one man[1] told him that a very good way would be that he (the minister) should appear to be annoyed with him and should send to command his presence, which mandate he would not obey, and on account of this act of disrespect he (the minister) should ordain that some punishment be inflicted, and at this aggravation he would leave the city and fly to Penagundy to stir up the King against the minister. He said that after he had gained the goodwill of the King he would so plot against him that he would render him disobedient; and that to give the King greater encouragement he would forge letters as if from captains which should contain the same counsel—namely, that he should leave that city where he was more prisoner than free—and would point out to him that he alone was king and lord, and yet that the land was under the power of Narasenaque his vassal, who had made himself very strong and powerful in the kingdom and held him (the King) prisoner, and had rebelled. He would urge the King to secretly quit the city and betake himself to a fortress belonging to the captain who had sent him that letter, and that there he should prepare himself, getting together a large following. And he would tell him that when the lords and captains came to know of his wish and determination they would act according to it, and would help him, and would come with him to fall upon Narsenayque, and would bestow upon him (Narsenaque) the prison in which he (the King) was now kept. So he would be king. (The captain further said) that after he had persuaded the King to this he would cause him to (leave the city), and while going out he would kill him, and that in this way Narsenaque should become king.

Narsenayque was well pleased to listen to this treason and to hear of the evil deed which this captain planned,

[1] Later on we learn that this man's name was Codemerade (p. 360).

and he showed him much favour. The captain disappeared after some days from where Narsenayque was, feigning to have fled; and he came to Penagumdy, where in a few days his arrival was known; and he set about and put in hand all those things that had been arranged. Every day he showed the King a letter, one day from a captain of one fortress, the next day another from another captain; and the King, understanding the plots contained in the letters so shown, replied that the counsel and advice seemed good, and yet how could he resist the power of Narsenayque, who, besides being minister of the kingdom, had (possession of) all the horses and elephants and treasure, so that he could at once make war against him? "True it is, Sire, that which thou sayest," answered the traitor, "and yet he is much misliked by all the captains who raised thee to be king, and as soon as they shall see thee in Chãodagary"[1] (which was a fortress whither he had advised him to flee, being one which up to that time was independent), "all will flock to thine aid, since they esteem it a just cause." Said the King,—"Since this is so, how dost thou propose that I should leave this place, so that my going should not be known to the guards and to the 20,000 men who surround me in this city?" "Sire," he replied, "I will disclose to thee a very good plan; thou and I will go forth by this thy garden, and from thence by a postern gate which is in the city (wall), and which I know well; and the guards, seeing thee alone without any following, will not know that it is thou, the King, and thus we shall pass to the outside of the city, where I will have horses ready that will take us whithersoever it seemeth good to thee." All this pleased the King well, and he placed everything in his hands; and, seeing fulfilled all his desire, the captain spoke with those men who

[1] Chandragiri, the capital of the kingdom in its decadent days.

guarded that part of the garden by which he wished that the King should fly, and which was near the King's own houses, (for into this garden the King often went to amuse himself with his wives, which garden was at that part guarded by a matter of 300 armed men) and to these men he spoke thus, saying to them :—" If ye shall happen to see me pass by here on such a night and at such an hour, and if ye shall see a man coming with me, slay him, for he well deserves it of me, and I will reward ye ;" and they all said that that would be a very small service to do for him. When that day had passed the traitor went to the King and said to him :—" Sire, do not put off till to-morrow that which thou hast to do to-day ; for I have the horses ready for thy escape, and have planned so to escort thee forth that even thy ladies shall not be aware of thy departure, nor any other person. Come, Sire, to the garden, where I will await thee." The King replied that his words were good and so he would do, and as soon as night was come and the hour arrived, the King went carefully out, and still more careful was he who for some time had awaited him ; and he gave signal to the armed men, and as soon as he was come to the garden he passed between two of them who were the guards, and they threw themselves on the King and slew him, and forthwith buried him at the foot of a tree in the same garden. And this being accomplished without their knowing whom they had slain, the traitor gave them his thanks, and returned to his inn to make ready to leave the city, and also so as not to give cause for talk therein. And the next morning it was found that the King was missing ; and though searched for throughout all the city no news of him could be heard, all the people thinking that he had fled somewhere, whence he would make war on Narsenayque. And to Narsenayque the news was straightway brought, and he, feigning much sorrow at it, yet made ready all his horses and elephants in case the kingdom should be plunged into some revolution by the death of the king; although as yet he knew not for certain how the matter stood, save that the King had disappeared. And afterwards the man came who had killed the King, and told him how it had been done and how secretly he had been slain, so that even the very men who had killed him knew not who it was; and Narsenayque bestowed upon him rich reward. And since there was no news of the King, and he holding everything now under his hand, he was raised to be king over all the land of Narsymga.

And this king left at his death five sons, one was called Busbalrao, and another Crismarao, and another Tetarao, and another Ramygupa and another Ouamysyuaya.[1]

And this Busbalrao inherited the kingdom at the death of his father Narsenayque and reigned six years, during which he was always at war, for as soon as his father was dead the whole land revolted under its captains; who in a short time were destroyed by that King, and their lands taken and reduced under his rule. During these six years the King spent, in restoring the country to its former condition, eight million gold *pardaos.* This King died of his sickness in the city of Bisnaga; and before he died he sent for Salvatimya, his minister,[2] and commanded to be brought to him his (the King's) son, eight years old, and said to Sallvatina that as soon as he was dead he must raise up this son to be

[1] Inscriptions do not give us the names of any sons having names like these. "Crismarao" probably represents Krishna Deva Râya, son of the first Narasa or Narasimha, and brother of the second Narasa, often called Vîra Narasimha.

[2] Sâluva Timma. This man belonged apparently to the new royal family, whose family name was Sâluva. He was the powerful minister of Krishna Deva Râya, but died disgraced, imprisoned, and blinded. He is constantly mentioned in inscriptions of the period.

king (though he was not of an age for that, and though the kingdom ought perhaps to belong to his brother Crisnarao) and that he must put out the eyes of the latter and must bring them to show him; in order that after his death there should be no differences in the kingdom. Salvatina said that he would do so and departed, and sent to call for Crisnarao, and took him aside to a stable, and told him how his brother had bade him put out his eyes and make his son king. When he heard this, Crisnarao said that he did not seek to be king, nor to be anything in the kingdom, even though it should come to him by right; that his desire was to pass through this world as a *jogi* (ascetic, recluse), and that he should not put his eyes out, seeing that he had not deserved that of his brother. Sallvatina, hearing this, and seeing that Crisnarao was a man of over twenty years and therefore more fit to be king, as you will see farther on, than the son of Busbalrao who was only eight years old, commanded to bring a she-goat, and he put out its eyes, and took them to show the King, for already he was at the last hour of his life; and he presented them to him, and as soon as the King was dead his brother Crisnarao was raised to be king, whose eyes the late King had ordered to be torn out.

CHAPTER V

Of the things done by King Crisnarao after he was raised to the throne.

As soon as Crisnarao was raised to be King and was obeyed throughout all his kingdom,—Salvatine being his minister, who had been the same for his brother Busbalrao,[1]—he without delay sent his nephew, son of

[1] Perhaps "Basava Râya," but as yet no brother of Krishna Deva is known bearing that name.

Busbalrao his brother, together with his own three brothers, to a fortress called Chãodegary; the nephew remained there till he died. And after the King had done this for his own safety he stayed in the city of Bisnaga for a year and a half without going outside of it, learning the affairs of the kingdom and looking at the testaments of past kings. Amongst these he found one of king Narsymga, whose minister his father Narsenayque had been, in which that King desired that his sons, or whoever should inherit this kingdom of Narsymga which he had gained by force of arms, should capture three fortresses that at his death remained in revolt against him, the which he had not himself taken because time failed him; one of them was called Rracholl,[1] and another Medegulla.[2]

Crisnarao, seeing this testament and seeing how badly the kings his predecessors had acted in what had been enjoined on them, determined at once to prepare armies and to go against these places; and one of these fortresses was called Odigair, and it belonged to the King of Orya. And, determining to go first against this, he collected (an army of) thirty-four thousand foot and eight hundred elephants, and arrived with this force at the city of Digary,[3] in which there were ten thousand foot soldiers and four hundred horse; for the fortress had no necessity for more by reason of its great strength, because it could not be taken except by being starved out.

And the King laid siege to it for a year and a half, in which time he made many paths across rocky hills, breaking up many great boulders in order to make a road for his soldiers to approach the towers of the fortress. The place at this time was so strong that they could not approach it except by one way which was so narrow that men could only pass along it one

[1] Raichûr. [2] Mudkal. [3] Udayagiri.

at a time; and in this place he made a broad road, and many others also, so that he could come close to the fortress.

And he took it by force of arms, and in it captured an aunt[1] of the King of Orya, who was taken captive and carried off with all the courtesy that he could show her, having her liberty; and he took her along with himself.

And after this was done he called Salvatinya and bade him see how well he had performed that which king Narsymga had by his testament enjoined on him, and yet he said he was not content with such a trivial victory, for[2] he desired to go forward a hundred leagues into the kingdom of Orya; and he ordered him to make ready provisions and pay fully the salaries of the forces.

And after this fortress was taken he departed and went against Comdovy,[3] which was one of the principal cities of the kingdom of Orya, and besieged it; and, learning this, the King of Orya came against him to defend his territories, and brought with him one thousand three hundred elephants, and twenty thousand horsemen, and he brought five hundred thousand foot-soldiers. Crisnarao, being aware of the approach of the king of Orya, left the city without assaulting it, saying that he preferred to fight the King in person and his army rather than to attack the city, and that there would be plenty of time afterwards to take it; and he went forward four leagues from it, leaving a force to prevent the escape of the people from the city if they should seek to flee to the coast. And he arrived at a large river of salt water crossed by a ford,[4] and on the other side of the river

[1] Some say uncle.

[2] In the MS. *em que avia* is evidently a mistake for *e que avia*.

[3] Kondavîd.

[4] I cannot identify this river. There is none such, to my knowledge, twelve miles or thereabouts from Kondavîd. "Salt" may perhaps mean brackish.

was the King of Orya with his army. King Crisnarao halted his army on this side of the river, and sent the King a message that if he desired to fight with him he would retire from the river two leagues, so that he (the king of Orya) might pass the river unmolested, and as soon as he had passed he would join battle; to which message the King of Orya gave no reply, but on the contrary made ready to give battle. And King Crisnarao, seeing his determination, crossed the river with all his forces and elephants, and in the crossing of the river there were heavy encounters on both sides, and many were slain. Notwithstanding this, King Crisnarao crossed the river, and on the bank fought so bravely that he defeated the King of Oria and put him to flight, in which defeat he took many horses and elephants.

And after the King had done this he told Salvatinea his minister that he purposed to turn back to the fortress, which had not yet experienced his strength, and he went against it, and stopped there two months besieging it; and he took it.

And he gave the command of it to Salvatinea, who left in it, from his army, for captain one of his brothers, in order that he himself might go forward with the King through the kingdom of Orya. And the King, passing the river once more in pursuit of the King of Orya, and taking and ravaging all the country which had no reason for expecting him, arrived at a city called Comdepallyr,[1] where were all the chiefs of the kingdom, it being the chief city in that kingdom. And he laid siege to it, and remained there three months without being able to capture it, and in the end he took it more by reason of his numbers than by force of arms; in which fortress he found many people of high rank whom he made captive, amongst whom was a wife of the King, and one of

[1] Kondapalle.

his sons who was a prince, and seven principal captains of the kingdom, all of whom he sent by road to Bysnaga.

And he went forward a hundred leagues into the kingdom, finding no one to bar his progress till he got to Symamdary,[1] which was a very large city, in which he halted for six months, waiting for the King of Orya. He sent many messages to say that he was waiting for him in the field, but he never came. And in this city he did many works, and gave alms to the temples, and erected therein a very grand temple to which he gave much revenue. And he commanded to engrave on it an inscription which says:—"Perhaps when these letters are decayed, the king of Orya will give battle to the King of Bisnaga. If the King of Orya erases them, his wife shall be given to the smiths who shoe the horses of the King of Bisnaga."

And after this was done he returned, leaving the greater part of those lands to the temples, and came to Bisnaga where he rested some days. And he sent to call the son of the king of Orya who was taken captive in the first fortress, and told him that as people said that he was a very active man and was very dexterous with both sword and dagger, he would be pleased to see him fence.

The young man said that since His Highness summoned him he would do what he could, and asked that this might be put off till next day. And when the next day came the King sent to call him, and also sent for one of his own men who at that time was very expert in the art,[2] that he should fence with him.

[1] Rajahmundry. The first syllable has been accidentally dropped, perhaps by the copyist.

[2] Senhor Lopes's "Chronica" has "*hũ homẽ seu que aquelle tempo d aquelle tempo muito sabia.*" Mr. Ferguson suggests, and with good reason, that for the second *tempo* we should read *jogo.* I have translated the passage accordingly. Senhor Lopes concurs.

And when the son of the King of Orya saw him, being offended with the King for sending a man to fight with him who was not the son of a King but only a man of humble birth, he cried out to the King:—"God forbid that I should soil my hands by touching a man not of the blood royal," and saying this he slew himself. And his father, hearing how his son was dead, wrote to Salvatinea (asking) by what means he could ransom his wife who remained in the power of the King, since his son was dead; to which he made answer that he should arrange the marriage of his daughter with the King, and that afterwards the King would restore him his wife and lands (or, would take only his lands).[1] This counsel he accepted, and he sent ambassadors to Bisnaga to arrange a marriage with his daughter, with which King Crisnarao was well content; and when the King of Orya knew his will (in the matter) he sent him his daughter; and with the coming of her they were friends. And Crisnarao restored the lands on the other side of the river, and kept those on the hither side for himself.

CHAPTER VI

How Crisnarao, after he had made peace with the King of Oria, determined to go against the land of Catuir.

AFTER Crisnarao had made peace, and had married the daughter of the King of Oria, and had restored to him his wife and the lands beyond the river, as has been narrated above, he made ready a large army

[1] The original MS. has *tomaria suas terras*—"would take his lands." Possibly the first of these words should have been *tornaria*, in which case the sentence would mean that the King "would restore the lands" to his enemy.

and prepared to attack Catuir,[1] which is the land of a lord who had been in revolt for fifty years; this land is on the Charamãodel side. And he went against it, and laid siege to one of the principal cities where the lord of the land was; and it is called . . .[2] and is surrounded with water.

Now at the time when Crisnarao attacked this city it was winter, for which cause the river that surrounded it was so swollen, and carried down so much water, that the king could do no harm to the place. And King Crisnarao, seeing this, and seeing that time was passing away without his attaining his desire, commanded his men to cut many new channels in order to be able to attack that principal (river) which had opposed itself to the fulfilment of his wishes. And this was done in a short time, since he had many soldiers; and after the (new) watercourses were finished and brought to where the water should go he opened mouths in the river, the water of which very soon flowed out so that the bottom could be seen, and it was left so shallow that it enabled him to reach the walls of the city; and the river was thus diverted into fifty different beds. Inside the city were one hundred thousand foot-soldiers and three thousand cavalry, who defended themselves and fought very bravely, but this availed little to prevent Crisnarao from entering in a few days and slaughtering all of them. He found large treasures in this city, amongst others in ready money a million and six hundred thousand golden *pardaos*, besides jewels, and horses, which were numerous, and elephants. And after he had finished the capture of this land Crisnarao divided

[1] I am unable to identify this country. The description of the town answers to Vellore in North Arcot, the fine old fort at which place is surrounded with a deep moat. According to tradition, this place was captured by Krishna Deva Râya from a Reddi chief.

[2] Blank in the original.

X

it amongst many of his captains, giving to each one what was necessary for him; and the chief who lived in the city and who was lord of the land was taken away captive and carried to Bisnaga, where he died in the King's prison.

And after the King had settled the country he came to Bisnaga, whence he sent Salvatinea to the city of Comdovy, since he was chief of it, by whom his brother was placed in it so as to see directly to the land and its government; for after the King returned from Orya he never went again thither.

And Salvatinea, having departed on his journey to Comdovy, before he arrived there, met, opposing his path, a Muhammadan named Madarmeluquo, who was a captain of the King on this side,[1] and who was awaiting him with sixty thousand men. Salvatinea had two hundred thousand men, and had very little fear of him; and with these he went against him, and took and defeated him, and took prisoners himself and his wife and son and horses and elephants and much money and store of jewels, and sent them all to King Crisnarao. The king commanded to put (the captives) in prison, and there they died. And Sallvatinea went to his territories, and after he had stayed there some months and seen to its government and decided matters in dispute, he returned to the King at Bisnaga, by whom he was well received as being the principal person in the kingdom.

[1] *Elrey Daquem.* This may be "the king on this side" or "the king of the Dakhan." The former seems most probable, and I think that the reference is to the forces of Sultan Qulî Qutb Shâh of Golkonda (see the Muhammadan account of affairs at this time, given above, pp. 132–135.)

CHAPTER VII

How Crisnarao, on the arrival of Salvatinia, determined to attack Rachol, a city of the Ydalcão, and to break the peace that had lasted so long; and the reason why.

AFTER Salvatinia had arrived and had been well received by the King, and after the lapse of some days, the King told him that he desired to fulfil all the wishes expressed in the testament of King Narsynga, one of which was to capture Rachol, which was a very strong city and amongst the principal ones of the Ydallcão, who had taken it from the kings his ancestors; and because there was now peace between both parties, and had been so for forty years, he knew not how he could manage to break it. But Salvatinia said that since the peace had been made under certain conditions—one of which was that if on either one side or the other any land-owners, captains in revolt, or other evil-doers should be harboured and their surrender should be demanded, they should forthwith be given up—there was now great reason for breaking the peace, since many land-owners and debtors to His Highness had fled into the kingdom of the Ydallcão. He counselled therefore that the King should send to demand the surrender of these men, and that on refusal to give them up there would be good ground for breaking the peace. Many, however, disagreed with this advice. Now it happened at this time that the King (of Bisnaga) sent Cide Mercar with forty thousand *pardaos* to Goa to buy horses, which Cide Mercar was a Moor in whom the King of Bisnaga confided on account of various affairs with which he had already been entrusted; and this man, when he arrived at a place where the Moors lived which was called Pomdaa and is two leagues from Goa, fled from that place, Pomdaa, to the Ydallcão, carrying with him all the treasure. Some say that the Ydallcão wrote to him a letter as soon as he got there. As soon as they gave to the King this news of the flight of Cide, and how he had carried off all the money, he said that he would write to the Ydallcão to send the man back to him with all the money, since he was his friend. Then the King caused a letter to be written, in which he spoke of the friendship that had existed for so many years so that nothing could shake it, and that he hoped that a traitor would not be the cause of breaking a peace of such long standing as had been between them; and he begged that he would send Cide back at once.

As soon as the letter was read to the Ydallcão he sent to summon his kazis and the men of his council, and he bade them read the letter which had come from the King, as to which letter there were many suggestions made. At the end of all they agreed that he should not send him (Cide) to him (the King of Bisnaga), for they said that he (Cide) was one learned in the law and related to Mafumdo.[1] And the Ydallcão, as a cloak to his action, gave Dabull to that Cide, by way of showing that he was not near his person nor knew he aught of him; from which town of Dabull Cide fled, nor had they any further news of him. When those who had come from the King returned bearing the Ydallcão's answer, the King showed great indignation at it, and held that the peace was broken; he at once ordered to appear before him the great lords of his Council, and had the letter read aloud so that all might hear. As soon as it was read he said that without more ado they should make ready, since he was determined to take full vengeance. But the councillors advised the King, saying that for such a small sum of money as this it was not well so to act; that he should think of what would be said and talked of throughout the world; and that if he

[1] Muhammad, Mahomet, *i.e.* he was of the Prophet's kindred.

was bent on breaking so prolonged a peace for such a trifling cause, he should call to mind that there never was any honesty in a Moor; that others were to blame in that which Cide had done; and that if Cide should dare to come to that war which was waged in order to take vengeance on him,[1] then it would be well that those who accompanied him should die, but that they knew that Cide would keep well away from the army.[2]

The councillors, however, saw that the King remained unmoved from his determination to make war, and they then counselled him, saying:—"Sire, do not go to war by that route (Dabull), but go against Rachol, which now belongs to the Ydallcão but of old was part of this kingdom; then the Ydallcão will be forced to come to defend it, and thus thou wilt take vengeance jointly both on one and the other." The King held this advice to be good and prepared for his departure, sending letters to Madre Maluco, and Demellyno, and Desturvirido,[3] and other superior lords, giving them an account of what had taken place in the matter of the Ydallcão, and how he had

[1] The text is confused here.

[2] The following is Barros's account of this affair of "Cide Mercar." After mentioning the terms of the treaty between Vijayanagar and Bîjapûr, one of which provided for the reciprocal extradition of criminals and debtors, he writes:—

"Crisnarao, knowing that he could catch the Hidalcão in this trap, called a Moor by name Cide Mercar, who had been in his service for many years, and bade him take forty thousand pardaos and go to Goa to buy horses of those that had come from Persia. Crisnaro wrote letters to our Captain . . . on purpose so that the affair might become widely known to all. Cide Mercar, either tempted by the large sum of money in his charge, or swayed by a letter which they say was sent to him by the Hidalcão, when he arrived at a *Tanadaria* called Pondâ, three leagues from Goa, fled to the Hidalcão from there. The Hidalcão as soon as he arrived sent him to Chaul, saying that he bestowed on him this *Tanadaria* as he was an honourable man of the family of Mahamed . . . ; but in a few days he disappeared from there, and they say that the king ordered his murder after he had taken from him the forty thousand pardaos."

[3] "Madre" stands for Imâd, the Bîrâr Sultan; "Virido" for the Barîd Sultan of Bîdar. I cannot explain *Demellyno* or *Destur*, unless the former be an error of the copyist for "Zemelluco" as written below, which certainly

determined to make war on him; from which lords he received answer that he was doing rightly, and that they would assist him as far as they were able. As to the Zemelluco, at the time when the messengers returned this answer he could find no excuse for not sending some troops to the aid of his sister who was wedded to the Ydallcão.

The King had sent the letters to those lords out of his great craftiness, for he told them of what he was about to do in order to seduce them to his side,—so far at least as concerned their goodwill, seeing that in the matter of troops he had no need of them—because if they had joined the Ydallcão he (the King) would never have conquered as he did; but because the Ydallcão was hated by them all as being a more powerful chief than they, (for there is little faith amongst the Moors, and they bite one another like dogs and like to see one after the other destroyed) he was conquered, as you will see hereafter, in the month of May, on the new moon day, in the year one thousand five hundred and twenty-two.[1]

After the King had made his offerings and performed sacrifices to his idols he left the city of Bisnaga with all his troops; and they marched in the following order. The chief of the guard (*o porteiro moor*)[2] led the advance with thirty thousand infantry—archers, men with shields, and musqueteers, and spearmen—and a thousand horse, and his[3] elephants. After him went Trimbicara with fifty thousand foot and two thousand horse and twenty elephants. After him went Timapanayque; he had

refers to the Nizâm Shâh. Several Portuguese writers omit the first syllable of "Nizâm" in their chronicles. On p. 348 below, these names are given as Madremalluco, Zemelluco, "Destuy" and "Virido;" and therefore "Destur" and "Destuy" must mean the Qutb Shâh of Golkonda, at that period Sultan Qulî. On p. 349 we have the form "Descar."

[1] For a full discussion of this date see above, p. 140.

[2] See above, p. 263, note. His name was Kâma Naik (p. 329).

[3] *Seus allyfantes.* Perhaps *seus* is a clerical error for *seis*, "six." Barros, in describing the same event, says "sixteen elephants."

with him sixty thousand foot and three thousand five hundred horse and thirty elephants; and after him went Adapanayque with one hundred thousand foot and five thousand horse and fifty elephants. After him came Comdamara,[1] and he had one hundred and twenty thousand foot six thousand horse and sixty elephants; after him went Comara, and he had eighty thousand foot and of horse two thousand five hundred, and forty elephants; after him the forces of Ogemdraho,[2] the governor of the city of Bisnaga, with one of his captains, who had one thousand horse and thirty thousand foot and ten elephants. After him went three eunuchs, favourites of the King, who had forty thousand foot and one thousand horse and fifteen elephants. The page who served the King with betel[3] had fifteen thousand foot and two hundred horse, but he had no elephants. Comarberca[4] had eight thousand foot and four hundred horse and twenty elephants. The people of the chief of Bengapor[5] went by another route with the people of Domar, who were very numerous; and in the same way went other captains of ten or twelve thousand men, of whom I make no mention, not knowing their names. The King took of his guard six thousand horse and forty thousand foot, the pick of all his kingdom, men with shields, archers, and three hundred elephants.

All were equally well armed, each after his own fashion, the archers and musqueteers with their quilted tunics,[6]

[1] See below, p. 360, note.

[2] Probably Ganda Râjah, brother of Sâluva Timma, the minister. (See p. 284, and note to p. 361.) The initial "O" may be the article "The."

[3] The great vassal lords of Madura, who after the fall of the kingdom established themselves as a dynasty of independent sovereigns, descended, so Barradas tells us, from the "Page of the betel" (above, p. 230).

[4] I think that the second *c* in this name is an error for *e*, and that "Comarberea" represents Kumâra Virayya of Mysore (above, p. 269). Later on Nuniz spells the name "Comarberya" (below, p. 336).

[5] Above, pp. 40, 60, 122.

[6] *Lades*, for *laudeis*, quilted tunics, doublets. The word is spelt in other places *laydes*, *lamdes*, *landys*, *lamdys*, and *landeis*. See note, p. 276, above.

and the shieldmen with their swords and poignards[1] in their girdles; the shields are so large that there is no need for armour to protect the body, which is completely covered; the horses in full clothing, and the men with doublets,[2] and weapons in their hands, and on their heads headpieces after the manner of their doublets, quilted with cotton. The war-elephants go with their howdahs (*castellos*) from which four men fight on each side of them, and the elephants are completely clothed, and on their tusks they have knives fastened, much ground and sharpened, with which they do great harm. Several cannon were also taken. I do not speak here of the washermen, who are numberless here—they wash clothes—nor of the public women who accompanied the army; there were twenty thousand of them with the king during his journey. Any one can imagine the amount of baggage that such a large number of people would take. In the rear with the king, but always on the road in front of him, some ten or twelve thousand men with water-skins who go seeking water, and place themselves along the road to give water to those who have no one to bring it to them; this is done so that none of the people should die of thirst. Three or four leagues in front of all this multitude go some fifty thousand men who are like scouts; they have to spy out the country in front, and always keep that distance; and on their flanks there are two thousand horse of the cavalry of that country. These are all bowmen, and they always advance on the flanks of the scouts.

In this order, as I have stated, they left the city of Bisnaga, and with them a great number of merchants,

[1] *Gomedares*, probably the modern *agomia* or *gomia*, "a poignard." Senhor Lopes refers me to Barros, Mendes, Pinto, &c., where the form used is *gumia*; the word being derived from the Arabic *kummiya*, which properly means a curved dagger—"*um punhal em meo arco*" (MS. in Portuguese, on Morocco, in Senhor Lopes's possession).

[2] See above, p. 276.

besides many others who were already in advance with all supplies; so that wherever you may be you will at once find all you want. Every captain has his merchants who are compelled to give him all supplies requisite for all his people, and in the same way they carry all other necessaries.

According to the King's custom, when he wishes to lie down and sleep, they make for him a hedge of brushwood and of thorns behind which his tent is pitched, which was done for him all along this route; on which route was seen a wonderful thing, namely that on passing a river which, when they reached it, came half-way up to the knee, before half the people had passed it was totally dry without a drop of water; and they went about in the sand of it making pits to find some water. In this order the King proceeded till he arrived at the town of Mollabamdym,[1] which is a league from the city of Rachol, where he pitched his camp so as to give a rest to the people after the fatigues of the march.

And the King being in the city of Mollabamdyn, settling all that was necessary for the siege of Rachol, there came to him people of the King of Bisnaga, and the people of Domaar, and also many other captains with an infinitude of people. As soon as they had joined and everything was put in order, and after his Brahmans had finished their ceremonies and sacrifices, they told the King that it was now time, that the pagodas had given sign of conquest, and that he should advance.

Then he sent the Moors in the royal service to lead the van, and Camanayque, the chief of the guard, pitched the camp very near the ditches of the city of Rachol, and every captain halted his people according to the commands given. The people of the city received them

[1] Malliâbâd, as now called, close to Raichûr. The name given by Nuniz I take to represent "Mallia (or Malliya) Banda," probably the Hindu name. *Banda* = "rock." "Malliâbâd" is the name given by the Musalmâns.

with many shots from heavy cannon that they had, and from many firelocks, and many arrows and musket-shots, so that those of the besiegers who arrived close to the ditches suffered heavily and wanted to retreat. But the King would not permit this, saying that he would not have sent them there were it not that he would soon effect an entry into the city, and if not, that they should all die; wherefore his men were compelled to attack the city, and did so in many brave and severe fights. In these many of them lost their lives, since those of the city were in very strong position and well acquainted with everything that was necessary for their defence, while the King's troops never ceased their attacks on the city. The captains, seeing how badly the attack was going in consequence of the number of soldiers killed, had recourse to lavish gifts and stratagems, as thus:—They began to buy (from the soldiers) the stones which they took from the walls and towers, and they paid them according to the value of the stone; so that the stones were worth ten, twenty, thirty, forty, and fifty *fanams*.[1] By this device they contrived to dismantle the wall in many places, and laid the city open; but since the city was in itself so strong, and the soldiers who were in it were such chosen men and so used to warfare, they killed many of the King's people. Yet not for that did they cease fighting, but every day and at every attack they became bolder, in consequence of their greed for what the captains gave them; for the money had the power of taking from them the terror of death which had inspired them before. They also gave them something for dragging away a dead man from the foot of the wall. So the fight dragged on for a space of three months till the Ydallcão came up with reinforcements.

Now I wish you to know more of the situation, and

[1] A small copper coin.

of the city, and the people which it held. This city of Rachol lies between two great rivers, and in the midst of a great plain where there are no trees except very small ones, and there are great boulders there; from each river to the city is three leagues. One of these rivers is the northern boundary, and beyond it the country belongs to the Ydallcão, and the other is the boundary to the south which is the boundary of Narsymga. This plain lies in the middle of these two rivers, and there are large lakes therein and wells and some little streams where the city is situated, and a hill which looks like a woman's breast and is of natural formation. The city has three lines of strong walls of heavy masonry made without lime; the walls are packed with earth inside, and it has on the highest point a fortress like a tower, very high and strong; at the top where the fortress stands is a spring of water which runs all the year round. It is held to be a holy and mysterious thing that a spring which is in a lofty situation should in some way never be without water. Besides this spring there are several tanks of water and wells, so that the citizens had no fear of being ever taken for lack of water; and there were in the city supplies for five years. There were eight thousand men as garrison and four hundred horse and twenty elephants, and thirty catapults (*trabucos*) which hurled heavy stones and did great damage. The towers which are on the walls are so close together that one can hear words spoken from one to the other. Between these and all around they posted their artillery, which consisted of two hundred heavy pieces, not to mention small ones. As soon as the people of the city knew of the arrival of the King's troops, and after they had received a captain of the Ydallcão who came with some soldiers to the city, they closed the gates with stone and mortar. The chief fight which takes place is on the east side, because on the north and south sides it stands on huge rocks which make it very strong; and, the city being besieged on all sides, the camp of the King was on the east side, and so was the strength of the attack.

CHAPTER VIII

Of the manner in which the King had his camp, &c.

THE tent of the King was surrounded by a great hedge of thorns with only one entrance, and with a gate at which stood his guards. Inside this hedge lodged the Brahman who washes him and has charge of the idol that he always carries about with him, and also other persons who hold offices about the King's person, and eunuchs who are always to be found in his chamber. And outside this circle all around are his guards, who watch all night at fixed spots; with this guard are quartered the officers of the household; and from thence to the front were all the other captains in their appointed posts, according as each one was entrusted and ordered. Outside of all these people, in a camp by themselves, were the scouts of whom I have already spoken, whose duty it is to patrol all night through the camp and watch to see if they can catch any spies. On the other side the washermen, (who are those that wash clothes) were in a camp by themselves, and they were near to the place where they could best wash clothes.

All the camp was divided into regular streets. Each captain's division has its market, where you found all kinds of meat, such as sheep, goats, pigs, fowls, hares, partridges and other birds, and this in great abundance; so much so that it would seem as if you were in the city of Bisnaga. And you found many endless kinds of rice, grains, Indian-corn, vetches (*minguo*),[1] and other seeds that they eat. Besides these things, which are necessaries, they had another (market) where you could find in great abundance everything that you wanted; for in these markets they sell things that in our parts are sold by professional hucksters.[2] There were craftsmen, also, working in their streets, so that you saw made there golden jewels and gewgaws, and you will find all kinds of rubies and diamonds and pearls, with every other kind of precious stone for sale. There also were to be seen sellers of cloths, and these were without number as that is a thing so many want, they being of cotton. There were also to be seen grass and straw in infinite abundance. I do not know who could describe it so as to be believed, so barren a country is this Rachol and so sandy. It is a mystery how there should be an abundance of everything therein. Any one can imagine what grass and straw would be required each day for the consumption of thirty-two thousand four hundred horses and five hundred and fifty-one elephants,[3] to say nothing of the sumpter-mules and asses, and the great numbers of oxen which carry all the supplies and many other burdens, such as tents and other things. Indeed no one who did not understand the meaning of what he saw would ever dream that a war was going on, but would think that he was in a prosperous city. Then to see the numbers of drums and trumpets, and other musical instruments that they use. When they strike up their music as sign that they are about to give battle it would seem as if the heavens must fall; and if it happened that a bird came flying along at the time when they made such a terrific noise, it used to come

[1] *Minguo*, probably *moong* or green grain ("Hobson-Jobson"). Ibn Batuta calls it *munj*, others *mungo*.

[2] *Regatoões d arte.*

[3] The total cavalry and elephants of the different columns enumerated above comes to 32,600 and 551 respectively.

down through terror of not being able to get clear of the camp, and so they would catch it in their hands; principally kites, of which they caught many.

But I cease to speak more of this because I should never finish; and so I turn to tell of the battle.

CHAPTER IX

How the King attacked the city of Rachol.

THE King, being as I have said at the siege of the city of Rachol, there came to him sure news that the Ydallcão had arrived at the river on the northern side, and that there he had pitched his camp. The King therefore sent his spies to keep watch over the foe, to see what he was doing and to send word of his every movement. With the coming of this news a tumult broke out in the camp, principally among the common soldiers, in whose minds suspicion was never wanting, and they still suffered under the terror inspired from old time by the Moors. There the Ydallcão halted some days so as to see what the King was doing and whether he would march to attack him there in his camp; for it was thought by him and by his people that as soon as the King should learn of his arrival he would at once march to meet him, and they decided that he could defend himself from the King in the place where he was better than in any other, by help of the river. For there was no other ford than the one close at hand; and this they proposed to guard so well that none should take it, least of all, they thought, men who (in their eyes) were only blacks.

Although the King heard that the enemy was on the opposite bank of the river, he yet made no move, nor did he do anything; and the Ydallcão, seeing that he made no advance, took counsel with his officers, and at this council the advice given greatly differed, as each had his own opinion regarding the non-movement of the King. Many said that this was because the King held his foe to be of little account, and wished to show his people how great was his power; and they said that he was only waiting for them to cross the river to at once fall upon them. The principal person who said this was Amcostam,[1] who was captain of Pomdaa at the time that Dom Guterre was captain of Goa.[2] Others said no, but that the King was afraid, thinking of times past and the many conquests that the Moors had gained over the Hindus, and that he had brought with him some veteran soldiers that had taken part in those wars. The advice of these was to push forward and pass the river. It was not well (they said) for the Ydallcão to show weakness, and the longer he stayed where he was the less would he benefit himself and harm the enemy; and although they were not so many in number as the Hindus, yet they had the advantage in the remembrance of the former battles that had been fought between them.[3] In the end the Ydallcão ordered that they should muster the forces, and said that after this was ended he would decide what was best to be done. When the muster was made, he found that he had one hundred and twenty thousand men on foot, archers and musqueteers and men with shields and spearmen, and eighteen

[1] Barros has *Ancostão*, and Correa *Ancoscão*. The latter termination seems the most natural—*cão* for *Khân*. The name appears to be "Ankus Khân." "Pomdaa" is Pomdâ or Pondâ, close to Goa.

[2] Dom Guterre de Monroy sailed from Portugal to India in 1515 in command of a fleet (Albuquerque, Hakluyt edition, iv. 194). In 1516 he was in command at Goa during the absence of Governor Lopo Soares at the Red Sea, between the months of February and September, and during that period attacked the Bîjapûr troops at Pondâ, which were commanded by Ankus Khân, with some success (Barros, Dec. III. l. i. c. 8). Osorio (Gibbs' translation, ii. 235) represents De Monroy as a man of a very cruel and licentious disposition. He was married to a niece of the governor.

[3] They believed, that is, that their prestige would give them great moral superiority over the Hindus.

thousand cavalry, and one hundred and fifty elephants; and when the muster was over and he had seen his forces for himself, seeing also the great strength of artillery that he had, he said that with his artillery he would seek to defeat the Rao of Narsymga. He therefore ordered them to make ready, since he desired to cross the river at once and advance to the attack; for the Ydallcão believed that his best course was to halt on the farther side and thence send his troops to charge the camp of the King, and that in so doing he would not be beaten and would not lose Rachol.[1]

In this greedy resolve he passed the ford and advanced to within three leagues of the King's camp, and he caused his own camp to be strengthened by large trenches, and commanded all his artillery to take post in front, and he arranged the order of his positions and the manner in which they should behave if they were attacked by the enemy. His camp extended along the length of the river for the sake of the water, that he might not be cut off from it by the enemy.

As soon as they brought news to the King that the Ydallcão had passed the river, he commanded all to make ready, but that no movement should take place in his army till he should see how the enemy acted; and when they brought him further news that the enemy had pitched his camp and strengthened his position, he ordered a general advance of all his forces. He divided his army into seven wings. Comarberya[2] begged from him (the command) of the van, he being the king's father-in-law and a great lord; he is King of Serigapatão and lord of a large state; he brought with him thirty grown-up sons. The King bade him pitch his camp a league from the Ydallcão and ordered all to arm themselves at dawn, as he intended then to give

[1] This passage is obscure.

[2] See above, p. 327 and note.

battle to the enemy; but the men of the Council said that that day was an unlucky day, and begged him not to attack, as it was a Friday, and they asked him not to attack till Saturday, which they hold for a lucky day.

When the King had left Rachol, those inside opened a gate, and one of the captains who was inside, a eunuch, made a sally with two hundred horse, certain foot-soldiers and elephants; he kept entirely along the river-bank on the King's flank. The object of this no one could guess, each one having his own opinion. As soon as the King halted he also did the same, keeping always his spies in the King's camp to see what passed and (what would be) the end of the battle. Since both armies were so close, each to his foe, they never put aside their weapons but watched all the night through.

Seeing that the dawn of Saturday was now breaking, the drums and trumpets and other music in the King's camp began to sound and the men to shout, so that it seemed as if the sky would fall to the earth; then the neighing and excitement of the horses, and the trumpeting of the elephants, it is impossible for any one to describe how it was. But even if told in simple truth it would hardly be believed the great fear and terror that struck those who heard it, so that even those very men that caused the noise were themselves frightened at it. And the enemy on their part made no less noise, so that if you asked anything you could not hear yourself speak and you had to ask by signs, since in no other manner could you make yourself understood. When all in the camp had gone to the front it was already two hours after sunrise, and the King ordered an advance of his two forward divisions, with command so to strike home that they should leave not one of the enemy alive; and this was forthwith done. They attacked the enemy so hotly that many of the King's troops found them-

Y

selves on the tops of the trenches[1] that the Moors had constructed in the fields. The Moors were disposed as if they expected that the King would engage them all at once with all his forces, and so it appeared to the Ydallcão and to his officers; and for that reason he held ready all his artillery, waiting for the time when, owing to the adventurousness of their main body, his men must of necessity cause much slaughter in their ranks. Then he intended to bring up his artillery and destroy them. But as soon as he saw the manner of their attack the Ydallcão had to abandon the plan that had seemed to him best for their safety, and he commanded the whole of the artillery at once to open fire; which discharge, as it was very great, did much damage to the enemy, killing many of the horse and foot and many elephants, and it compelled the King's troops to retire. As soon as the Moors saw their enemies beginning to leave the field they charged all amongst them, so that there did not remain one man in the saddle nor one who kept his face to the foe; but all the King's troops began to fly, and the Moors after them, slaughtering them for about half a league. When the King saw the way in which his troops fled he began to cry out that they were traitors, and that he would see who was on his side; and that since they all had to die they should meet their fate boldly according to custom.[2] "Who ranges himself with me?" he cried. Immediately there thronged about him all those lords and captains that were ready to side with him, and the King said that the day had arrived in which the Ydallcão would boast that he had slain in it the greatest lord in

[1] The original has *cavas e baudes*. The meaning of the last word is not clear.

[2] *Avyão de morrer pedido ausa da morte*. *Ausa* is perhaps for *ousadia*, "boldness;" and the passage would then mean that since death appeared inevitable they should meet it half-way, and not lazily await it; they should die like soldiers in a charge, not stupidly standing still to be slaughtered.

the world, but that he should never boast that he had vanquished him. Then he took a ring from his finger and gave it to one of his pages, so that he might show it to his queens in token of his death, that they might burn themselves according to custom. Then he mounted a horse and moved forward with all his remaining divisions, commanding to slay without mercy every man of those who had fled. As soon as these last saw what a reception they received at the hand of their fellows they felt compelled to turn and charge the enemy, and their attack was such that not one amongst the Moors was found to face them; for the Moors met them as men engaged in a pursuit, all in great disorder. The confusion was so great amongst the Moors and such havoc was wrought (in their ranks) that they did not even try to defend the camp they had made so strong and enclosed so well; but like lost men they leaped into the river to save themselves. Then after them came large numbers of the King's troops and elephants, which latter worked amongst them mischief without end, for they seized men with their trunks and tore them into small pieces, whilst those who rode in the castles (howdahs) killed countless numbers.

The troops advanced thus, pursuing the foe, till the King reached the river, where, seeing the death of so many—for here you would see women and boys who had left the camp, there horses and men who through clinging one to another could not escape as there was so much water in the river—and the King's troops stood on the bank, so that whenever a man appeared he was killed, and the horses that tried to clamber up by the bank of the river, unable to do so, fell back on the men, so that neither one nor the other escaped, and the elephants went into the stream, and those that they could seize were cruelly killed by them. Seeing what passed, I say, the King out of compassion commanded the troops to retire, saying that numbers had died who did not deserve death nor were at all in fault; which order was at once obeyed by all the captains, so that each one withdrew all his forces.

The King then advanced to the camp of the Ydallcão and rested himself in his tent, but many of the captains spoke against his action in thus taking repose, saying that he ought rather to complete the destruction of all his enemies, and they would secure this for him; and that if he did not wish himself to do this he should at least command some of them to do it, and that it was not wise to cease from pursuit so long as daylight should last. To whom the King answered that many had died who were not to blame; that if the Ydallcão had done him wrong, he had already suffered enough; and moreover, that it did not seem to him good, since Rachol remained behind them to be taken, that they should go forward, but rather they should make themselves ready for its capture; for that the siege had to be conducted henceforth in a new and better manner. For the King was persuaded throughout that, since the Ydallcão had lost so many men and so much honour, and had lost indeed all his power, he would not wish to live any longer, and that he must be dead on the field. Which, however, was not so, seeing that the Ydallcão had not even entered into the fight, but had all the time remained under guard of Sefallarym[1]—he who now calls himself Açadacão and is lord of Belgaum—who, fearing the event, contrived by cunning that the Ydallcão should select him for his guard with all his troops, among whom he had four hundred cavalry; and when he saw how the soldiers fled, and how completely they

[1] "Sufo Larij," Barros, Dec. III. l. iv. cap. 5. Asada Khân's love of intrigue was proverbial amongst the Portuguese of that day.

had been defeated, he said to the Ydallcão, "Sire, if thou seekest to live follow me!" and the Ydallcão took refuge on an elephant and followed him, leaving his camp and all that he possessed. And as Açadacão wished him to travel by land,[1] he took no care to search for the ford, but skirting the range of hills on the south he went by that way.[2]

As it may be asked what became of the captain who sallied out of Rachol with the two hundred horsemen and elephants and foot-soldiers, I say that he ever kept himself advised of what passed in the field; and as soon as he learned that the Ydallcão was defeated he turned back to take refuge again in the citadel. But those within were not of a mind to receive him, there being a quarrel between him and another captain who was in the city; and he, seeing that they would not admit him, was forced to think how he could save himself, and he did so by passing the river by another ford farther down, and so saved himself. The belief of many was that he who was inside thought that he would now possess the city for his own, and that he would thereby become rich, and for that reason refused to receive the captain.

CHAPTER X

Of the spoil taken from the Moors, of how the King burned all the dead, and of what Christovão de Figueiredo did.

THE King being thus in the camp, he commanded the spoil that remained of the Moors to be collected, and there were found five captains who were taken prisoners (those of highest rank were found amongst

[1] *Como quer que Açadacão trazia quem hia a terra.* A doubtful passage.

[2] *Tomamdo a falldra da serra da bamda do sul.* It would be interesting to learn which range of hills is referred to.

the dead); the chiefest of them was Salabatacão,[1] who was captain-general of all the troops of the Ydallcão. He had taken for his guard in the battle five hundred Portuguese of the renegades who were with the Moors; and as soon as this Salabatacão saw that his army was defeated, he strove to collect and form a body of men, but could not do it because there was not one amongst them who thought of aught but to save himself. And thinking it worse to be conquered than to die, he threw himself amongst the King's troops, slaughtering them, and doing such wonderful deeds that ever after he and his Portuguese were remembered, so much were their terrible strokes feared, and the deeds they did; so that they let them pass on, and they penetrated so far amongst the troops that they found themselves close to the King's bodyguard. There the horse of Salabatacão was killed. In order to succour him the Portuguese did great deeds, and killed so many men that they left a broad road behind them which no one dared to enter, and they fought so well that they got another horse for Salabatacão. As soon as he was on its back he seemed like nothing but a furious wolf amongst sheep; but since already they were all so exhausted, so wounded all over, and so encircled by the enemy (for they were attacked at every point), Salabatacão was at length overthrown, and his horse with him. And as the Portuguese who tried to succour him were all killed, not one escaping, and he himself was wounded in many places, he was taken prisoner.

The spoil was four thousand horses of Ormuz, and a hundred elephants, and four hundred heavy cannon, besides small ones; the number of gun-carriages for them was nine hundred, and there were many tents and pavilions. I take no account of the sumpter-

[1] Salâbat Khân.

horses and oxen and other beasts, for they were numberless, nor of the numbers of men and boys, nor yet of some women, whom the King ordered to be released.

Here the King stayed till all the dead had been burned, and the customary honours had been paid to them; and here he gave much alms for the souls of those who had been killed in battle on his side. These numbered sixteen thousand and odd. These things done, he turned again upon Rachol and pitched his camp as he had done before.

During this return of the King there came to meet him Christovão de Figueiredo,[1] who was at that time in the city of Bisnaga with horses, and he took with him twenty Portuguese musqueteers, he also himself having his musquet. The King took much pleasure in his company, glad that he should see the war and his great power; and he ordered some tents to be given to him of those taken from the Ydallcão, and commanded that he should be lodged close to his own quarters. One day Christovão de Figueiredo told the King that he wanted to go and see the city, but the King said that he should not set his heart upon that because he did not want any disaster to befall him. But Christovão de Figueiredo replied that the whole business of the Portuguese was war, and that this would be the greatest favour that he could do him, namely that His Highness should permit him to go and see the Moors. So the King gave him leave and sent some people with him. Christovão de Figueiredo went close to the trench before the walls, keeping himself as much concealed as possible, and seeing how fearlessly the Moors exposed themselves on the wall, began, with the musqueteers whom he had brought, to open fire on them in such a way that he slew many,

[1] See above, p. 251, note.

the Moors being careless and free from fear, as men who up to then had never seen men killed with fire-arms nor with other such weapons. So they began to forsake the wall (at this point), and the king's troops found an opportunity of coming in safety to it, and they began to destroy much of the masonry; and so many people collected on this side that all the camp was put in commotion, saying that Christovão de Figueiredo had entered the city with his Portuguese. This was told to the King. Those in the city could not understand what was going on, nor how these people came to be in the King's service, until they recollected how on the day of the other fight the Portuguese had come, and then they considered themselves lost. For by the aid of those men the King's people came without fear to the wall, where already it was damaged in many places, because the city had its cannon so high up that these could do no injury to the men who were at the foot of the wall. The wall also was filled up inside with earth, and there were no cannon in the breaches. The people of the city whom up to that time they had killed had been supplied with stones which they had flung on the besiegers from the top of the wall, and with musquets and arrows, so that even if the King's men were able to reach the wall at all they were at least wounded; but as Christovão de Figueiredo with the Portuguese prevented the enemy from appearing at all on the wall, the Hindus were enabled to reach it at their ease.

Here you would have seen how the King's captains begged Christovão de Figueiredo to permit them one day to attack the Moors in his company, and he, in order to content the more honourable of them, went with them on those days. One day he divided his musqueteers into three companies and began to kill several amongst the Moors who showed themselves,

RAICHUR FORT

(*From a Photograph by* F. DUNSTERVILLE, Esq.)

insomuch that none durst be seen; and then the King's troops began, in these three divisions, to attack the wall with many pickaxes and crowbars,[1] and he sent to tell the rest that they should attack on their own account; and such was the result that the defenders of the city began to abandon the first line of fortification, and the women and children took refuge in the citadel. The captain of the city, seeing the dismay that had spread amongst his people, began to turn them back with encouraging words, and with some of them betook himself to that part of the wall which he saw was most severely pressed, begging them that they would come back to the wall and not be afraid. He was answered by some that at that point were those Franks[2] who were helping, and that as soon as any one showed himself he was a dead man; and he, wishing to see for himself where the Portuguese were, reached over with his body in front one of the embrasures and was killed with a musquet-shot that struck him in the middle of his forehead. It was said by the Moors that Christovão de Figueyredo had killed him, and they took notice of him (*derão sygnaes d elle*). As soon as the captain was thus killed there was great lamentation in the city, and soon the wall was deserted, so that the men from the King's camp were left to do as they pleased with it; and they noticed the outcry that arose within and saw that there was no one defending the wall. They therefore retired to see what should happen, and left off fighting for that day.

1 *Llavãocas*, for *alavanca*, a Portuguese word for crowbar still used everywhere in Ceylon.

2 *Framges*, *i.e.* Feringhees, Franks, or Europeans.

CHAPTER XI

How those in the city asked for terms, and the king granted them quarter.

NEXT day, which was twenty days since the battle had taken place in which the Ydallcão had been defeated, the men of the city opened a gate, and with a white flag carried in front of them went the way of the King's camp with their hands uplifted, begging the King's mercy.

When the King was advised of their coming, he commanded Solestema,[1] his minister, to receive them; and when they saw that he came out to receive them they began to hope that they should experience kindness at the King's hands.

Thus they came to the place where he was, and there they prostrated themselves on the ground with much groaning and tears, and besought his pity and benevolence.

The King commanded them to rise, saying that he would save all their persons and property, and that they need have no fear but should return to the city, and that on the next day he would enter it; and he bade a captain take possession of the city.

Whilst the Moors were thus in presence of the King (the soldiers looking on), they saw Christovão de Figueiredo, and told the King that the conquest and capture of the city was due to that foreigner, that he had slain their captain, and with his people had killed many Moors, which caused the city's destruction. The King, casting his eyes on Christovão de Figueiredo, nodded his head, and turned to the people telling them to observe what great things could be

[1] Sâluva Timma.

effected by one good man. He then retired to his tent and the men of the city to the city, and the king's troops made great feasting and rejoicing.

CHAPTER XII

How the King entered the city, and of the feast that was made for him, and of the regulations and arrangements he made there.

As soon as the next day dawned, the King, after he had performed both his customary prayers and others which it is their wont to offer after victories, giving thanks to God (for indeed the principal thing they pray for is a conquest such as this), rode in company with the other great lords and his captains, and with his guard took the way to the city. There the citizens were standing awaiting his arrival, with more cheerful countenances than their real feelings warranted, yet striving to take courage, and they followed him with much loud shouting; crying,—"God be praised who has sent to save us after so many years!" and with these and other such words they begged him to spare them and have pity on them. So he proceeded till he arrived close to the citadel, when he sent to call the most honoured men in the city, and to these the King said that he would spare all their property, that they might freely act as they wished regarding both that and their persons, and those who wished to stay in the city might remain in their old state as before; and as for those who wished to depart they might do so at once with all that they possessed. They all raised their hands to Heaven, and threw themselves on the ground in thankfulness for such gentle treatment. While the King was thus engaged there came men to tell him that his troops were robbing the city, and he at once took measures to prevent this, and everything was returned to its owner; but as in such cases as these the conquered are content merely with their own liberty, laying little store by anything they may get back, great robberies took place; and some of these afterwards came to the ears of the King, and those who had done it were soundly chastised.

In a short time the defeat of the Ydallcão was known all over India, and also in other regions of the interior, he being a great lord in these parts; and as soon as the news was carried to Zemelluco and Madremalluco and Destuy and Virido, and also to other lords who were like slaves to the king Daquym,[1] although in some measure they rejoiced since they wished him ill, yet on the other hand they began to be fearful for their own safety.[2] So they all took measures to send their envoys, and these found the King still inside the city of Rachol. Astonished though they were to see that the King had captured so strong a city, they were much more surprised to see how great was his power and how numerous his troops. Having arrived where he was they gave him the letters they had brought, and these were forthwith read. In these the chiefs told the King that he ought to content himself with having defeated the Ydallcão as he had done, and ought not to wage further war; they begged him of his goodness to return to the Ydallcão that which he had so taken from him, and that if he did so they would always obey whatever he commanded; but if he was not of a mind to this, then he must know for certain that they would be compelled to turn against him and forthwith

[1] Rey Daquym, *i.e.* King of the Dakhan. This evidently refers to the Bâhmanî king, who was still recognised as titular sovereign, though the whole country had revolted and broken up into five independent kingdoms. For the names that precede this see note to p. 325 above.

[2] *Começarão deitar as barbes em remolho.* This refers to the Portuguese proverb—"Quando vires arder as barbas do teu vizinho, põe (or deita) as tuas em remolho"—"When you see your neighbour's beard on fire, steep your own in water;" or guard against like treatment.—D. F.

join the Ydallcão, for whom they would speedily recover that which he had now lost. The King, seeing what was contained in the letters, answered them in the following manner by one single letter to them all;— "Honoured Madremalluco, and Zemelluco, Descar, and Veride, and all others of the kingdom of Daquym, I have seen your letters, and thank you much for what you have sent to say. As regards the Ydallcão, what I have done to him and taken from him he has richly deserved; as regards returning it to him that does not seem to me reasonable, nor am I going to do it; and as for your further statement that ye will all turn against me in aid of him if I do not do as ye ask, I pray you do not take the trouble to come hither, for I will myself go to seek ye if ye dare to await me in your lands;— and this I send you for answer." And he commanded to give many gifts to the messengers, and giving his letter to them sent them away.

CHAPTER XIII.

How a number of people left the city, and the King did much kindness to them.

MANY people left the city, and to many who had nothing wherewith to depart the king commanded to give all that was required for their journey. Here the King stayed some days, after having made all the arrangements that were necessary for the government of the city; and after repairing the walls he left behind him sufficient troops to guard the place, and took the road to the city of Bisnaga, where he was received with great triumphs, and great feasts were made and he bestowed bountiful rewards on his troops.

As soon as the festivals were ended he went to the new city; and, being there, they told him how there was entered an ambassador of the Ydallcão. Already he knew that an ambassador had come but he pretended that he did not know, since it is not customary for the King to send out to receive any ambassador (on his arrival). Since this ambassador was in the city of Bisnaga, knowing that the King was in the new city, which is two leagues from Bisnaga, he betook himself thither; and close to the city bade the people pitch his tent, which was the best and most beautiful and rich that up to that time had ever been seen in those parts. This ambassador was called Matucotam; he brought with him one hundred and fifty horse and much people to serve him and many pack animals, among which were certain camels. He brought also two of the scribes of the chamber of the Ydallcão, so that indeed you would believe that he had brought all the power of the Ydallcão "pera segumdo elle ficou desbaratado."[1]

As soon as he had thus settled himself the ambassador sent to inform the King of his arrival, and begged that His Highness would grant him an audience and despatch him without delay. The King replied that he would see him,[2] but told him that he should not be impatient since he himself had but now arrived, and that he would give him leave to depart as soon as the time had arrived. And with this the ambassador stayed there a month without the King having sought to see him, nor having asked to know why he had come; he went every day to the palace, and seeing the way in which the King acted towards him he determined to speak no more but to wait till the King summoned him. Still he never ceased to go every day to the palace and to speak with the nobles. One day the King sent to tell the ambassador that the following day was an auspi-

[1] This passage appears to be corrupt, and I have been unable to guess at its meaning. Senhor Lopes, whom I have consulted, is equally at fault about it.

[2] *Elrey o mamdou ver.*

cious day, and that he wished to hear him and learn wherefore he had come, and the ambassador made ready as it behoved him to present himself before so great a lord. As was fitting, considering his mission and the request he had to make, he was accompanied by many Moors whom the city contained, and had with him all his people with their trumpets and drums as was customary; and so he went to the palace, where he was received very honourably by the nobles and officers of the household. They seated themselves inside the first gate, awaiting there a message from the King giving permission to enter where he was, and there was no long delay before the command to admit him was given. His obeisance to the King having been made according to his mode and custom, the men of the council standing by the King's side, he was bidden to announce the terms of his embassy, the King being ready graciously to listen; and the ambassador, seeing that the King so commanded, delivered himself of his message in manner following, with the awed demeanour assumed by such envoys when they find themselves in presence of such great kings.

CHAPTER XIV

How the Captain acquitted himself of his embassy before the King.

"SIRE! the Ydallcão, my master, sends me to thee; and by my mouth he begs thee that thou wouldest be pleased to do justice. He bids me say that he bears very good will towards thee[1] as towards the most true and powerful prince in all the world, and one possessed of most justice and truth; that thou without reason hast broken the friendship and peace which thou hast had

[1] *Que elle te ama a ty diante de ty.* The latter words may be an emphatic expression, akin to *diante de Deus e de todo o mundo,* "In the face of God and all the world."

towards him, and not only so but a peace which was made so many years ago and maintained by all the kings so truthfully; that he does not know why thou hast left thy kingdom and made such war on him; that he was without suspicion when they brought him the news how thou hadst besieged the city of Rachol, and hadst robbed and destroyed the country round about, which news caused him to move and come to its rescue; that then all the members of his court were slain by thee, and his camp all plundered and destroyed, thou thyself being good witness of what was done, and that he begs thee to make amends therefor, and to send back to him his artillery and tents, his horses and elephants, with the rest that was taken from him, and also to restore his city of Rachol; that if thou wilt give him the satisfaction for which he prays as to this property and all other things thou wilt have him always for a loyal friend; but if not, thy action will be evil, even though pleasing to thyself." Thus he ended, without saying more. The King said that he might retire and repose, and that next day he would give him leave to depart, and the King gave him a robe of silk and the cloths that are customary.

CHAPTER XV

How the King sent to call the ambassador, and of the answer which he gave to him.

NEXT day the King sent to call the ambassador, and after other things had been spoken of between[1] them, the King said that he would be content to restore everything to the Ydallcão according to his wish, and would be pleased at once to release Salabetacão, provided the Ydallcão would come and kiss his foot. When the

[1] *Ante elles* should be "*antre elles.*"

ambassador heard the King's answer he took leave of him and went to his tent; and he wrote to the Ydallcão and told him what had passed, sending to him one of the scribes that had come with him. And much time had not passed when the Ydallcão sent him a reply, saying: How could it be possible for him to meet the King, seeing that he could not go to Bisnaga? and yet that he was of full mind joyfully to do that which the King wished. With this answer the ambassador went to the King, and since the King would have set higher value on the Ydallcão's coming to kiss his feet than on all that he had taken from him, he said to the ambassador, "Do thou cause the Ydallcão to come to the confines of my kingdom, for I shall be soon there." Agreeing to this, the ambassador departed, so as to persuade the Ydallcão to come to the boundary. The King on his part went forthwith to a city called Mudugal[1] which is close to the boundary, and there he waited until they told him that the Ydallcão was coming and was already near at hand. Forthwith the King set out to meet him, and entered the kingdom of Daquem, so desirous was he to meet the Ydallcão; but the Ydallcão, after all, dared not meet the King. And the King journeyed so far, whilst they kept saying to him, "Lo! he is here close at hand," that he even went as far as Bizapor,[2] which is the best city in all the kingdom of Daquem. It has numbers of beautiful houses built according to our own fashion, with many gardens and bowers made of grape-vines, and pomegranates, and oranges and lemons, and all other kinds of garden produce.

Hither went the King, for it seemed well for him to await the coming of the Ydallcão in so goodly a city; and he formed the determination that if he got him here he would seize him or command him to be put

[1] Mudkal. [2] Bîjapûr.

to death, to avenge the affront that had been put upon him; and seeing that his enemy did not dare to come he remained in the city several days. Then he turned away because water failed him; for since this city lies in a plain and has no water save that which it receives from rainfall into two lakes, of which there are two large ones, the Moors had opened these in order to drain them, so that the King should not be able to stay in their country. For this reason it behoved the King to depart. But the city was left almost in ruins—not that the King had commanded it to be destroyed, but that his troops, in order to make fires for cooking, had torn down so many houses that it was a great grief to see—and this was occasioned by there being in the country a dearth of firewood, which comes to them from a great distance. The Ydallcão sent to ask the King what wrong the houses of his captains had done that he had commanded to destroy them; for there remained no other houses standing save only the palaces of the Ydallcão, the King himself being therein. The King sent answer that it was not he who had done it, but that he could not control his people.

When the King went to the town of Modogal the Ydallcão returned to Bigapor, where, seeing the great havoc that had been wrought in it, he took to himself the blame for such damage having been done,[1] saying that if he had gone to the King such destruction would not have taken place, and that at least he could do this in future; he said that he had been badly advised since for his own part he had been prepared to do it. Thus he took counsel with his advisers, putting before them how secure his position was if he had the friendship of the King, that if allied to him he might be able to still further increase (the greatness of) his State, and that

[1] *Todo a cullpa de tall ser feyto por asy.* Lit. "all on account of his having acted thus."

with the King's favour he would be able to carry out all his wishes. Concerning these things and others similar to these he continued constantly speaking with his advisers. Wherefore Açadacão the lord of Bilgao, he who had fled with him in the battle, and who was a man sagacious and cunning in such matters, addressed the Ydallcão begging permission to go himself to the King, and saying that he would remedy everything and would cause everything to take place just as his lord wished; and the Ydallcão listened to him readily.

Now Açadacão did not trouble himself to make this journey because he desired to serve the Ydallcão, for another would have done it as well, but he did it with a villanous motive and from the ill-will he bore to Salebatacão whom the King held in prison at Bisnaga; and the reason that he had this wicked motive was because Salebatacão knew that Açadacão was the man that had caused the Ydalcão to flee, and that the cowardice of such an act was enough to destroy an army. Salebatacão had spoken angrily about this to all those who went to see him or who were sent to visit him, and he always said that he did not desire to be released from his captivity save for one reason only, namely that he might ruin Açadacão and war against him as against a mortal enemy. These things were all known to Açadacão, and he knew that if they released him it would come to pass as he had said, and therefore he determined to prevent this by contriving his enemy's death, as will be mentioned in its place. It was for this reason that Açadacão asked to be sent as ambassador to the King; and this was done.

CHAPTER XVI

How Açadacão went as ambassador for his King and compassed the death of Sallabatecão.

Açadacão, being despatched by the Ydallcão, accompanied by certain horsemen with some servants took the road to the city of Mudogal where the King was, and the Ydallcão went with him as far as the river. When Açadacão had arrived, being allowed inside the city by command of the King, he remained several days without seeing the King until he was summoned by his order; then he was admitted and spoke with the King, giving him, with the manner of one who in such negotiations is both wise and bold, an excuse for the mistake which the Ydallcão had committed. He knew how to speak to the King so well that he removed all the King's wrath and fury against the Ydallcão, and he told the King that the principal cause why the Ydallcão did not meet him was the conduct of Salebatacão whom he had captured, and that this man had written to the Ydallcão telling him not to do so, and giving for reason that the King desired to slay him. By these and other similar sayings he sought to set the King's mind against Salebatacão, even to the death, and the King, seeing what Açadacão wanted, and believing that a man of such great fame would not be guilty of saying anything that was not perfectly true, angrily commanded that Salebatacão, who was then in Bisnaga, should be beheaded; and this was at once done as soon as the message arrived.

As soon as Açadacão had accomplished this business he thought himself unsafe, and at once asked leave of the King, saying that he wished to go and get the Ydallcão to come to the river, so that when His Highness arrived he might meet him there. But the King told him not to be impatient but to amuse himself there some days, and added that he wished to show him some things, and that he had somewhat about which to speak to him. Açadacão, however, being afraid that his treason would be discovered, did not feel safe, and behaved in such a manner that what he had done concerning Salebatacão was found out; wherefore the King sent to seize him, but when they went to look for him he was already gone. For he fled one night and betook himself to the Ydalcão, telling him that the King had commanded Salebatacão to be put to death, and that he wanted to do the same to him, and so he had escaped; and it seemed to him that he (the Ydalcão) ought not to trust the King, who after all was nothing but a black. After he had spoken in this way he went to Bilgao, where he strengthened his position, and when the Ydallcão sent afterwards to summon him he never obeyed, because he knew that the wickedness that he had done had been found out.

CHAPTER XVII

How the King went to the extremity of his territory to meet the Ydalcão, and what he did on not finding him.

THE King did not fail to go to the extremity of his territory, and since he did not find the Ydalcão there, nor his mother, as Açadacão had told him, he at once perceived that this was due to trickery on the part of Açadacão, and that he had done it all in order to compass the death of Salebatacão. Full of fury at this he entered the kingdom of Daquem and marched against the city of Culbergura[1] and destroyed it and razed the fortress to the ground, and the same with many other places.

Thence he wanted to press forward, but his council-

[1] Kulbarga, the ancient Bahmanî capital.

lors did not agree to this, saying that water would fail him by that road and that it did not seem to them that those Moorish lords whom they counted as friends would be otherwise than afraid that the King would take their lands as he had taken those of the others, since they all served one sovereign, and that for this reason these lords would probably make friends with the Ydalcão, and together they would come against the King; and although there was no reason to be afraid of them, yet the King must needs fear the want of water, of which they had none. And the King agreed that this counsel was good.

In this city of Calbergara, in the fortress belonging to it, the King took three sons of the King of Daquem. He made the eldest King of the kingdom of Daquem, his father being dead, though the Ydallcão wanted to make King one of his brothers-in-law, who was a bastard son of the King of Daquem, and had married one of the Ydallcão's sisters; for this reason he had kept these three brothers prisoners in that fortress. He whom he thus made King was received by all the realm as such, and obeyed by all the great lords, and even by the Ydallcão owing to his fear of the King.[1] The other two brothers he took with him, and gave them each one an allowance, to each one every year fifty thousand gold *pardaos;* and he holds them and treats them as princes and great lords, as indeed they are. After the return of the King to Bisnaga, which took place in the same year in which he had left, nothing more passed between him and the Ydalcão worthy of record, relating either to peace or war.

[1] This passage does not seem very exact from an historical standpoint (see above, p. 157, and note).

CHAPTER XVIII

How this King, during his own lifetime, raised to be King his son, being of the age of six years.

AFTER the King had made an end of this, and had obtained so great a victory over his enemies, perceiving that he was already advanced in years, desiring to rest in his old age and wishing his son to become King when he died, he determined to make him King during his lifetime, the boy being six years old and the King not knowing what would happen after his death. Wherefore he abdicated his throne and all his power and name, and gave it all to his son, and himself became his minister, and Salvatinica[1] who had held that office became his counsellor, and he made one of the latter s sons a great lord among them. And so far did King Crisnarao go that after he had given the kingdom to his son, he himself did obeisance to him. With these changes the King made great festivals which lasted eight months, during which time the son of the King fell sick of a disease of which he died.

After his death Crisnarao learned that his son had died by poison given him by the son of Sallvatinica, and in his anger, being certain that this was so, he sent to call Salvatinica and his son and Guandaja, brother of Ssallvatinica, and many other captains relatives of Ssallvatinica, and made them a speech at the time of the salaam, there being present many chiefs and principal persons of the kingdom, and relations of Ssallvatinica; he addressed him thus:—"I held thee always as my great friend, and now for these forty years thou hast been governor in this kingdom, which thou gavest me; yet I am under no obligation to thee for that, because in doing so thou didst act in a way contrary to thy duty. Thou

[1] Sâluva Timma.

wert bound, since thy lord the King my brother commanded so, to put out mine eyes; yet thou didst not carry out his will nor obey him, but instead thou didst cheat him and the eyes of a goat were put out, wherefore, since thou didst not fulfil his command, thou wert a traitor, and thy sons with thee for whom I have done so much. Now I have learnt that my son died of poison given to him by thee and thy sons, and for that ye are all here made prisoners." With these words he arose and laid hands on them and seized them, and in doing so called for aid from many Portuguese who were then in the country with horses, asking them to come to his aid; and after he had seized the men, father and sons, they remained three years in prison. And he made minister a son of Codemerade, the same who had killed the son of King Narsymga in the city of Penagundy in the garden by treachery, by command of the King his father, as has already been told in this history.[1]

And soon afterwards Danayque, son of Salvatinica, escaped from prison and betook himself to a mountain range in which dwelt nobody but robbers and highwaymen, and in this there was a fortress where dwelt a captain, his relative, who received him and helped him in all that he could, and from there he made such war on the King Crisnarao that he was driven to send against him much people, and as captain of the army

[1] (Above, p. 310 f.) The original text has "*e fez regedor hũu filho Codemerade,*" but I cannot identify the name with any ordinary Hindu name or title; and if "son of Codemerade" be meant, as I suppose, the *de* has been omitted accidentally. If, however, there has been a confusion of syllables and the original reading was "*filho de Codemera,*" then I would point to the list given above of powerful nobles (p. 327) who commanded the forces of the king in the great Râchol campaign, one of whom was called *Comdamara.* In the concluding paragraph of this chapter we have this new minister's name given as "Ajaboissa," and in the list of provincial lords (p. 385 below) as "Ajaparcatimapa." The latter name sounds more probable than the former. The first half would be the family name, the last, "Timmappa,' his own personal name.

he sent his minister Ajaboissa, who invested the place on all sides and took him therein and brought him prisoner to the King. After he had so come the King commanded him to be brought before him, with Sallvatinica his father and another brother of his who was kept in the prison, and he sent them to the place of executions and there had their eyes put out, for in this country they do not put Brahmans to death but only inflict some punishment so that they remain alive. So he put them in prison again, and there Timadanayque died, and Salvatinica his father remained in the prison with his other son Gamdarja.[1]

CHAPTER XIX

How the Ydallcão came against Rachol, and did not dare to await the King, and fled.

At this time the Ydallcão collected his army and formed afresh his forces of cavalry and elephants, and marched upon Rachol which remained under the king of Bisnaga. Hearing this news, Crisnarao, without even telling any one, ordered to saddle a horse, and he rode at full speed in the direction of Rachol where already the Ydallcão was; but as soon as his enemy was aware of the coming of the King he fled. On the road King Crisnarao bought six hundred horses from the Portuguese at the rate of $4\frac{3}{4}$ for 1000 *pardaos*.[2] And from Rachol he sent a message to the Ydallcão saying that

[1] In the passage earlier in this chapter Sâluva Timma is said to have had a brother "Guandaja." Putting the two together, it would seem that his brother and son both bore the same name, probably Ganda Râjah. Paes refers to the brother as being in his day governor of the capital (above, p. 284). He calls him "Gamdarâjo." See also p. 327, note 2.

[2] *Cymco menos huũ quoarto por mil pardaos*, or nineteen for four thousand pardaos. The chronicler was a trader in horses at Vijayanagar. Later on he mentions the usual price as twelve or fifteen horses for a thousand *pardaos* (below, p. 381).

he had already twice broken his oath and his word, and that as he had not fulfilled the promise he had made he would make war on him in such fashion as that by force he should become his vassal, and that he would not let him alone till he had taken from him Billgao.[1]

As the winter had now begun the King could not then go forward, and so he went to Bisnaga to make ready for this war; and he commanded to prepare a large force of artillery, and sent an ambassador to Goa to ask for the help of the Governor. He promised him that after taking Billgao he would give him the mainland; for this city of Billgao is fifteen leagues from Goa, and its captain is lord of the mainland of Goa. Goa is the frontier or boundary of his city of Billgao, and there is one of his captains at a fortress called Pomda which is three leagues from Goa by the mainland, who also receives the revenues and has command over several villages; and in like manner these and others have captains appointed by the Ydalcão, who is lord of the whole land.[2]

While Crisnarao was thus making ready he presently fell sick of the same illness of which all his ancestors had died, with pains in the groin, of which die all the kings of Bisnaga.

Now this King Crisnarao, when he was young and growing up in this city of Bisnaga, had an intrigue with a courtezan for whom he had much affection, and who was called Chinadevidy, and for the great love he bore her he promised many times that if ever he became King he would marry her; and though he said this in jest, it afterwards became true, so the history records. For when raised to the throne and taken away from the things he had done when a young man, he still did not forget the affection he felt for this woman, but used

[1] Belgaum.

[2] The captain of Pondâ was Ankus Khân (above, p. 335, notes 1, 2).

A GATEWAY IN THE FORT OF VIJAYANAGAR

secretly to leave his palace and go to her house. And this was discovered one night by his minister Sallvatinica, who watched him until he had got into the woman's house, and he rebuked him much for it and brought him back to the palace. Then the King told him how well he loved her, and that he had promised to marry this woman and was determined to do so in any case; and the minister, seeing how he was bent on it, gave way to his wish, saying that he would accomplish it in such a way that His Highness would not be blamed for it. In order to do this he sought for him a very beautiful woman of the family of the kings of Narsymga, and after he had married him to her, at the end of the wedding ceremonies, he put this woman and the other in a house, to which he had added a tower very lofty and large, and in which he lodged her. Afterwards the King married many other wives, for these kings hold it as a very honourable thing to have many wives; and this King Crisnarao married four, and yet he loved this one better than any of the others. This King built a city in honour of this woman, for the love he bore her, and called its name Nagallapor and surrounded it with a new wall which is one of the best works that he has in his kingdom, and he made in it a street very long and large with houses all of masonry. In order to people this town he ordered all the chiefs of his kingdom to build themselves palaces therein, and so they did. This town has one principal street, of length four thousand and seven hundred paces[1] and of breadth forty, which is certainly the most beautiful street it is possible to see; and he made and finished this town without stinting any expense on it. It now yields forty-two thousand *pardaos* of duties for things which enter into it, the duties in

[1] About a mile and a quarter. Nágalapúr is the modern Hospett. If the measurement is accurate, this street, leading, no doubt, towards the capital, is now non-existent.

this land being very great; since nothing comes through the gates that does not pay duty, even men and women, as well as head-loads and all merchandise.

This King also made in his time a lake for water, which lies between two very lofty *serras*. But since he had no means in the country for making it, nor any one who could do it, he sent to Goa to ask the Governor to send some Portuguese masons, and the Governor sent him João della Ponte,[1] a great worker in stone,

[1] The Della Pontes are more than once mentioned in the history of the sixteenth century. They were probably an Italian family, or Italian in origin, and engineers by profession, the Rialto at Venice having been constructed by Antonio della Ponte in 1588. This, however, may be a fanciful connection. It is possible that both in Portugal and in Italy families may have received that surname in consequence of their skill in bridge-building, or of one of the family having in former days distinguished himself by the construction of a particular bridge. The engineer mentioned in the text is probably the individual who at the end of April 1520 was sent by the king of Portugal to examine into the possibility of building a fortress at Tetuan in Morocco. Dom Pedro de Mascarenhas (afterwards, in 1554, Viceroy at Goa) sailed on this mission from Ceuta, and "João Nunes del Pont" is mentioned as accompanying him. The king and the Emperor Charles V. were both at this time anxious to prevent the Moorish corsairs from using Tetuan in future, as they had done in the past, as a base for their piratical attacks on Spain and Portugal. (Damião de Goes, *Chronica de Dom Manuel*, edit. of Coimbra, 1790, vol. i. Part IV. p. 532; *Alguns documentos do Archivo Nacional da Torre do Tombo*, Lisbon, 1892, pp. 445-446.)

In 1521, some time after the month of March, when Dom Diogo Lopes de Sequeira, the governor of Goa, had returned from his expedition to the Red Sea, he was urged by his counsellors to build a fortress at Madrefabâ near Goa, as the place contained an anchorage sufficient for an entire fleet. (Correa, *Lendas da India*, ii. p. 622.) Correa continues: "The governor, however, thought better to send in a *cotia* Antonio Correa and Pero de Coimbra, his chief pilot, to inspect the river of Madrefabâ and measure the water on the bar, and Manuel da Ponte, Overseer of Works, and João de la Ponte, his brother, who understood it well, to view the land, and if there were stone, and if lime could be made for the work, and to bring him certitude of all."

If this man were the same as he who went with Mascarenhas to Tetuan, he had, in all probability, not been long in India when he went to Madrefabâ. This seems to show that the great tank of Krishna Deva Râya, seen in process of construction by the chronicler Paes (see p. 244), and mentioned in the text by Nunez, was not begun till at least the autumn of 1521. If so, Paes did not *write* his description of Vijayanagar till after that date (say 1522). (See above, p. 162.)

to whom the King told how he wanted the tank built. Though it seemed to this man (*mestre*, modern *maistry*) impossible to be made, nevertheless he told the King he would do it and asked him to have lime prepared, at which the King laughed much, for in his country when they build a house they do not understand how to use lime. The King commanded to throw down quantities of stone and cast down many great rocks into the valley, but everything fell to pieces, so that all the work done in the day was destroyed each night, and the King, amazed at this, sent to call his wise men and sorcerers and asked them what they thought of this thing. They told him that his idols were not pleased with this work, it being so great and he giving them nothing, and that unless he spilled there the blood of men or women or buffaloes that work would never be finished. So the King sent to bring hither all the men who were his prisoners, and who deserved death, and ordered them there to be beheaded; and with this the work advanced. He made a bank across the middle of the valley so lofty and wide that it was a crossbow-shot in breadth and length, and had large openings;[1] and below it he put pipes by which the water escaped, and when they wish so to do they close these. By means of this water they made many improvements in the city, and many channels by which they irrigated rice-fields and gardens, and in order that they might improve their lands he gave the people the lands which are irrigated by this water free for nine years,[2] until they had made their improvements, so that the revenue already amounts to 20,000 *pardaos*.

Above this tank is a very large ridge all enclosed, and in the middle some very strong gates with two towers, one on one side and one on the other; and

[1] *Espaços*. This probably means sluices or weirs.
[2] *Por nove anos de graça.*

within are always posted 1000 men on guard. For through this gate all things must enter that come into the two cities, since in order to enter the city of Bisnaga there is no other road but this, all other roads meeting there. This gate is rented out for 12,000 *pardaos* each year, and no man can enter it without paying just what the renters ask, country folk as well as strangers. In both these cities there is no provision or merchandise whatever,[1] for all comes from outside on pack-oxen, since in this country they always use beasts for burdens;[2] and every day there enter by these gates 2000 oxen, and every one of these pays three *vintẽes*,[3] except certain polled oxen without horns, which never pay anything in any part of the realm.

Outside these two cities are fields and places richly cultivated with wheat and gram and rice and millet, for this last is the grain which is most consumed in the land; and next to it betel (*betre*), which is a thing that in the greater part of the country they always eat and carry in the mouth.

CHAPTER XX

How on the death of Crisnarao his brother Achetarao was raised to be king.

BEFORE[4] the death of King Crisnarao from his disease as has been before recounted, being sick and already

[1] *Não ha nenhũ manimẽto nem mercadaryas.*

[2] The original (itself a copy) has "*nesta terra não se servem de bestas pera carreguas.*" I think that the words *se não* must have been accidentally omitted before *de bestas*, and have ventured so to render the passage.

[3] About $3\frac{1}{2}$d. (?). A *vintem* is about $1\frac{7}{20}$d.

[4] I have given the meaning here, not a literal translation. The writer begins: "After the death of King Crisnarao from his disease, as has been already recounted." Then he inserts a long parenthesis which might be read: "While he was sick . . . he had made a will . . . &c. . . ." down to . . . "but only one of the age of eighteen months." Then he continues: "After his death (as I have said) Salvanay became minister," &c. . . .

despairing of his life, he made a will, saying that of his three brothers whom, at the time when they raised him to be King, he had sent to be confined in the fortress of Chamdegary[1] with his nephew, son of the King Busbalrao,[2] they should make King his brother Achetarao[3] who now reigns; for the latter seemed to him to be better fitted for that than any of the others, for the reason that he himself had no son of fit age for the throne, but only one of the age of eighteen months. After his death Salvanay became minister of the kingdom, and governed it till the coming of King Achitarao from the fortress of Chamdegarŷ where he was detained. And he further left in his will that he should take Billgao,[4] and should make war on the Ydallcão.

Which King Chytarao, after he ascended the throne, gave himself over to vice and tyranny. He is a man of very little honesty, and on account of this the people and the captains are much discontented with his evil life and inclinations; for he has never done anything except those things that are desired by his two brothers-in-law,[5] who are men very evilly disposed and great Jews. By reason of this the Ydalcão, learning of how little weight he was, determined to make war on him, believing that he would easily succeed since the King was not inclined to war; so he made his forces ready, and began to invade the King's territory, and arrived within a league of the city of Bisnaga. Chetarao was in the city with such great forces and power that he could easily have captured him if his heart had allowed him to take action, since the Ydallcão had with him

[1] Chandragiri.

[2] See above, p. 315.

[3] Achyuta.

[4] Belgaum.

[5] These two may perhaps be two of the three powerful brothers Râma, Tirumala, and Venkatâdri, of whom the two first married two daughters of Krishna Deva. In such case, however, they would not have been actually brothers-in-law of King Achyuta, but of his brother the late king.

only 12,000 foot and 30,000 horse; yet with this small force the Ydallcão entered Nagallapor a league from Bisnaga and razed it to the ground. The King never tried to go out against him, nor had he the stomach for a fight, and there were only small skirmishes by some captains, good horsemen. These spoke to the King, asking that His Highness would give them leave to attack, and saying that his own presence was unnecessary for so slight an affair; but the King was terrified, and by the advice of his brothers-in-law (of which they gave not a little) decided to send and make peace with the Ydallcão. The Ydallcão was very glad and made a peace with him which was to last for a hundred years, on condition that the King should give him ten *lakhs* of gold *pardaos*, each *lakh* being 100,000 *pardaos*, and further should yield up to him the city of Rachol which the King Crisnarao had taken from him, and which had a revenue with its lands of 150,000 *pardaos*, as well as jewels which could easily be valued at a *lakh*. The King accepted these terms, and the Ydallcão departed well pleased with this money; and after all was done the King sent to him a diamond stone weighing 130 *mangellinis*,[1] with fifteen other similar ones worth fully a *lakh*. This money he soon afterwards recovered and put in his treasury, exacting payments from his captains and people so ruthlessly that they say that in six months he had recovered and put the whole in his treasury.

Wherefore the captains and troops, both because he made this peace and because he exacted this sum of money contrary to the wishes of them all, have lived greatly discontented, and have held that if this kingdom should ever be brought to destruction, it

[1] A mangelin is roughly equivalent to a carat, but actually the difference is one-fifth; 4 mangelins = 5 carats. So that 130 mangelins = 162 carats. The *Koh-i-nur*, when brought to England, weighed 186 carats. (See Appendix A.)

must take place in the lifetime of King Chitarao; for he had destroyed the principal people of his kingdom and killed their sons and taken their goods, all owing to the bad counsel of his brothers-in-law, by whom he was dominated.

I will tell you of one who was called Crisnaranarque whom he seized one night, and who, before he surrendered himself, killed all his wives, in number two hundred, and then killed himself with poison in presence of the King. This was because the King wanted to kill his son in his presence. By sale of the captain's arms, namely daggers, swords, spears, battle-axes and other things, which were all ornamented with gold and silver, the King realised more than 3000 *pardaos*. In this way the kingdom has been deprived of its principal men and of those who sustain it, wherefore the Ydalcão holds it in so little esteem that he puts upon it every day a thousand affronts and requisitions. Of this King there is nothing more so far to recount, save that he is a man that they hold to be of little force of character, and very negligent of the things which most concern the welfare of his kingdom and State.

CHAPTER XXI

Of the manner of attendance on these kings, which is as follows.

[What follows concerns the reign of Achyuta Râya.]

ALL the service of this house, with the things which they make use of, is of silver and gold, that is to say basins and bowls, stools, ewers, and other vessels of that sort. The bedsteads[1] in which his wives sleep are covered and adorned with silver plates. Every wife has her bed in which she sleeps, and

[1] The word used is *catre*, a light bedstead, probably the origin of the modern South Indian word "cot," for a camp bedstead.

2 A

that of the King is plated and lined and has all its legs of gold, its mattress of silk, and its round bolster worked round the ends with large seed pearls. It has four pillows of the same pattern for the feet, and has no other sheet than a silk cloth on top. He always carries with him a mosquito curtain with a frame of silver,[1] and he has a house made of pieces of iron in which is contained a very large bed, which is intended for such time as he takes the field.

He has five hundred wives and as many less or more as he wants, with whom he sleeps; and all of these burn themselves at his death. When he journeys to any place he takes twenty-five or thirty of his most favourite wives, who go with him, each one in her palanqueen with poles. The palanqueen of the principal wife is all covered with scarlet cloth tasselled with large and heavy work in seed-pearls and pearls, and the pole itself is ornamented with gold. The palanqueens of the other wives are ornamented only with silver, but another palanqueen, which is for his own person, always goes on the right side, and is in the same way decorated with gold. For a son or a daughter, if such an one goes with him, he takes another bedstead of ivory inlaid with gold; and when he takes the field, wherever he pitches his camp there they make for him houses of stone and clay, for he does not stay in a tent, and he always has these decorated with cloths.[2]

[1] *Arquelha de prata. Arquelha* is a mosquito-net. Since manifestly the net itself could not be made of silver, the allusion is probably to its supports. Senhor Lopes, in a letter to me, suggests that it means the upper portion of the canopy, "*le ciel du lit*," or the framework that holds the curtains, *arquelha* being a diminutive of *arco*, a "bow" or "arch." In this case it might mean the domed ceiling of a canopy made in Muhammadan fashion, and the curtains may have been of silk or brocade, and not of mosquito-netting.

[2] The word used is *armadas*. It may mean "furnished" or "hung round with cloths," or possibly "fenced" or "fortified."

In his palace within the gates he is served by women and eunuchs and servants numbering fully five or six hundred; and these wives of the King all have their own officials for their service, each for herself, just as the King has within the gates, but these are all women. The palaces of the King are large and with large rooms; they have cloisters like monasteries, with cells, and in each one is one of his wives, and with each of these ladies is her maid-servant; and when the King retires to rest he passes through these cloisters, and his wives stand at the doors and call him in; but these are not the principal wives, they are the daughters of captains and nobles of the country. Inside the gates of the palace they say that there are over two hundred milch-cows, from the milk of which they make butter for these ladies to eat.

The King has no expense in connection with his food, because the nobles send it to him every day to his house, namely rice and wheat and meat and fowls with all other necessary things. In the kitchen there are some two hundred inferior guards, and four over it, and two chief officers of the guard; and those who are now captains of the guard of this king are called, one Pedanayque and the other Ajanaique, they are also captains of soldiers; these porters do not go further inside than through four or five doors, because inside of these are none but eunuchs and women.

When the King rides out there go with him usually two hundred horsemen of his guard whom he pays, and a hundred elephants, and this in addition to the captains, forty or fifty in number, who are always in attendance with their soldiers. He takes with him two thousand men with shields, all men of good position, ranged in order on the flanks, and in front goes the chief *alcaid* with about thirty horsemen having canes in their hands like porters; the chief *alcaid* bears a different wand; he who is now the chief *alcaid* of this King is called Chinapanaique. Behind with the rearguard goes the Master of the Horse with two hundred horsemen, and behind the cavalry go a hundred elephants, and on their backs ride men of high estate. He has in front of him twelve destriers, saddled, and in front of these horses go five elephants, specially for the King's person, and in front of these elephants go about five-and-twenty horsemen with banners in their hands, and with drums and trumpets and other music playing so loudly that you can hear nothing. Before these goes a great drum carried by men at the sides, and they go now and then striking it; the sound of this is heard a long distance off; and this drum they call *picha*. After the King has mounted he counts the two hundred horsemen and the hundred elephants and the shield-bearers of the guard, and whoever is missing is severely punished and his property confiscated.

CHAPTER XXII

Of the manner in which obeisance is done to the King, &c.

THE manner of the salaam which the nobles make to the King every day is this:—In the morning the nobles go to the palace at ten or eleven o'clock, at which hour the King comes out from within where his wives are, and after he has taken his seat they open to the nobles, and each one comes by himself and bows his head and raises his hands. This is what they call the "salaam" (*salema*). With the king are about ten or twelve men who have the duty, on the entrance of each captain, of saying to the King: "See, your Highness, your captain so-and-so, who makes salaam to you."

The Kings of Bisnaga have always liked, for show, to have many horses in their stables, and they always had eight or nine hundred horses and four or five hundred elephants, on account of which, and on account of the people that looked after them, they were put to great expense; and this King that now is (Achyuta Râya) has in his stable seven hundred and odd horses and four hundred elephants. He spends on account of them and for their attendants, to whom he gives food, two thousand gold *pardaos* per day. And of horsemen whom the King pays he has six thousand, and all of them are on the stables establishment (?) (*comem da estrebarya*); and those who serve them are paid each year, some a thousand *pardaos*, some five hundred, some three hundred, and those who have less pay receive not less than a hundred. Of these six thousand, two hundred are obliged to ride with the King.

The kings of this country are able to assemble as many soldiers as they want, as they have them there in their kingdom and have much wealth wherewith to pay them. This King Chitarao has foot-soldiers paid by his nobles, and they are obliged to maintain six[1] *lakhs* of soldiers, that is six hundred thousand men, and twenty-four thousand horse, which the same nobles are obliged to have. These nobles are like renters who hold all the land from the King, and besides keeping all these people they have to pay their cost; they also pay to him every year sixty *lakhs* of rents as royal dues. The lands, they say, yield a hundred and twenty *lakhs* of which they must pay sixty to the King, and the rest they retain for the pay of the soldiers and the expenses of the elephants which they are obliged to maintain. For this reason the common people suffer much hardship, those who hold the lands being so tyrannical. Of these sixty *lakhs* that the king has of revenue every year he does not enjoy a

[1] *Seus leques* must be a misprint for *seis leques.*

larger sum than twenty-five *lakhs*, for the rest is spent on his horses, and elephants, and foot-soldiers, and cavalry, whose cost he defrays.

During his feasts and the almsgiving to his temples all these captains, who are thus like renters, must always attend the court, and of those whom this King always has about him and by whom he is accompanied in his court there are more than two hundred. These are obliged always to be present with the King, and must always maintain the full number of soldiers according to their obligations, for if he finds that they have a less number they are severely punished and their estates confiscated. These nobles are never suffered to settle themselves in cities or towns because they would there be beyond reach of his hand; they only go thither sometimes. But a concession is granted to the kings that are subject to him, namely they do not go to court unless they are summoned, and from their own cities they send to him their rents or tributes; yet the King of Bengapor is obliged to be always in camp, and he goes to court twice in the year.

The kings who are subject are these, besides this King of Bengapor, namely the King of Gasopa and the King of Bacanor and the King of Calecu and he of Batecala,[1] and these when they come to the Court of Bisnaga are not held in higher esteem than any other captains, either by the King or by the other nobles.

The captains and lords of this kingdom of Bisnaga, as well those who are at Court as those who are away from it, have each one his secretary who goes to the palace in order to write to him and let him know what the King is doing; and they manage so that nothing takes place of which they do not soon know, and day and night they are always in the palace. And the King also, when he leaves the palace, takes with him on his

[1] Above, pp. 121, 281, and notes.

own account secretaries, who write what the King says, and the favours he bestows, and with whom he spoke, and upon what subject, and what his determination was; and to these men is given a credit equal to that of the Evangelists, because they say that whenever the King speaks there must be something worthy to be recorded, and also that such a record is necessary for their remembrance. Thus no written orders are ever issued, nor any charters granted, for the favours he bestows or the commands he gives; but when he confers a favour on any one it remains written in the registers of these secretaries. The King however gives to the recipient of the favour a seal impressed in wax from one of his rings, which his minister keeps, and these seals serve for letters patent.

These Kings of Bisnaga eat all sorts of things, but not the flesh of oxen or cows, which they never kill in all the country of the heathen because they worship them. They eat mutton, pork, venison, partridges, hares, doves, quail, and all kinds of birds; even sparrows, and rats, and cats, and lizards, all of which are sold in the market of the city of Bisnaga.

Everything has to be sold alive so that each one may know what he buys—this [1] at least so far as concerns game—and there are fish from the rivers in large quantities. The markets are always overflowing with abundance of fruits, grapes, oranges, limes, pomegranates, jack-fruit, and mangoes, and all very cheap. It is said that in the markets they give twelve live sheep for a *pardao*, and in the hills they give fourteen or fifteen for a *pardao*. The King drinks water which they bring from a spring, which is kept enclosed under the hand of a man in whom the King has great confidence; and the vessels in which they draw the water come covered and sealed. Thus they deliver it to the women who wait on

[1] *E ysto he coanto a caça.* At the present day in Southern India game-birds are sold alive, generally with the eyes sewn up.

him, and they take it inside to the other women, the King's wives.

The greatest mark of honour that this King of Bisnaga confers on a noble consists of two fans ornamented with gold and precious stones, made of the white tails of certain cows;[1] he gives them bracelets also. Everything which the noble receives is placed on the ground. The King confers very high honour, too, if he permits a certain one to kiss his feet, for he never gives his hands to be kissed by any one. When he wishes to please his captains, or persons from whom he has received or wishes to receive good service, he gives them scarves of honour[2] for their personal use, which is a great honour; and this he does each year to the captains at the time that they pay him their land-rents. This takes place in the month of September[3] when for nine days they make great feasts. Some say that they do this in honour of the nine months during which Our Lady bore her Son in the womb; others say that it is only done because at this time the captains come to pay their rents to the King. Which feasts are conducted in the following manner.

The first day they put nine castles in a piece of ground which is in front of the palace, which castles are made by the nine principal captains in the kingdom. They are very lofty and are hung with rich cloths, and in them are many dancing-girls and also many kinds of contrivances. Besides these nine every captain is obliged to make each one his castle, and they come to show

[1] This evidently refers to the yak-tail whisks used in the service of idols in the temples and in the palaces of nobles. On occasions of ceremony at the present day any chief or noble who has a pretension to sovereignty, or who claims descent from a line of independent lords, proclaims his dignity by the use of certain insignia, and amongst these the yak-tail fan finds place. It is one of the most graceful of ornaments. The soft white hair is set in a metal handle of brass or silver and waved slowly by an attendant. Its material object was to keep away flies.

[2] *Pachari* for *pichhauri*.

[3] Above, p. 263.

these to the King. Each one has his separate device, and they all come like this during the nine days of the feast. The officers of the city are bound to come with their devices each day at night, just as in our festivals, and in these nine days they slaughter animals and make sacrifice. The first day they kill nine male buffaloes and nine sheep and nine goats, and thenceforward they kill each day more, always doubling the number; and when they have finished slaying these beasts, there come nine horses and nine elephants of the King, and these come before the king covered with flowers—roses—and with rich trappings. Before them goes the chief Master of the Horse with many attendants, and they make salaam to the King. And when these have finished making their salaam there come from within priests, and they bring rice and other cooked edibles, and water, and fire, and many kinds of scents, and they offer prayers and throw the water over the horses and elephants, just (as our priests do with) holy water; and they put chaplets of roses on them. This is done in the presence of the King, who remains seated on a throne of gold and precious stones; he never sits on this except only this once in the year. And this King that now reigns does not sit on it, for they say that whoever sits on it must be a very truthful man, one who speaks the whole truth, and this King never does so. Whilst this is going on there pass by the King fully a thousand women, dancing and posturing before him. After all the devices that have been prepared have been witnessed all the horses of the King pass by, covered with their silken trappings,[1] and with much adornment of gold and precious stones

1 "Silken trappings." The original word is *patollas*. Later on (see p. 383), in describing the king's dress, Nuniz writes, "*os seus vestidos sao pachõiis*," &c. Both these words probably refer to the same Canarese word, *paṭṭuda*, "a silk cloth." Barbosa and Pinto use it in the form *patola*, Correa as *patolo*, and Peyton (in Purchas) as *patolla*. (Yule and Burnell's Glossary, *s.v. Patola*.) In Telugu, *pattu* = "silk."

on their heads, and then all the elephants and yokes of oxen[1] in the middle of the arena[2] in front of the palace. After these have been seen there come thirty-six of the most beautiful of the King's wives covered with gold and pearls, and much work of seed-pearls, and in the hands of each a vessel of gold with a lamp of oil burning in it; and with these women come all the female servants and the other wives of the King, with canes in their hands tipped with gold and with torches burning; and these then retire inside with the King. These women are so richly bedecked with gold and precious stones that they are hardly able to move.

In this way during these nine days they are compelled to search for all things which will give pleasure to the King.

The King has a thousand wrestlers for these feasts who wrestle before the King, but not in our manner, for they strike and wound each other with two circlets with points[3] which they carry in their hands to strike with, and the one most wounded goes and takes his reward in the shape of a silk cloth,[4] such as the King gives to these wrestlers. They have a captain over them, and they do not perform any other service in the kingdom.

And after these nine days are finished the Rao[5] rides out and goes to hold a review of the troops of his captains, and he goes a length of two leagues be-

[1] *Juntas.* The meaning is doubtful, but in all probability yokes of oxen are referred to. In the Canarese country these are often handsomely decorated and clothed when attached to travelling vehicles.

[2] *Terreiro.*

[3] *Rodas de bicos.* These may perhaps have been weapons such as in England were known as "knuckledusters."

[4] A free translation. The original runs, "*de maneira que o que fica de baixo d outro mais ferido vay, leva a fogaça, que he hũu pacharim,*" &c. It seems curious that the vanquished should be rewarded. *Leva a fogaça* is literally "takes the cake." For *pacharim* see above, p. 376, note 2.

[5] This is the only occasion on which the chronicler gives the king his hereditary title of *Râya*, usually spelt *Rao* by the Portuguese. *Râya* is the same as *Râja.*

tween the armed men. At the end he dismounts and takes a bow in his hand and shoots three arrows, namely one for the Ydallcão, and another for the King of Cotamuloco,[1] and yet another for the Portuguese; it was his custom to make war on the kingdom lying in the direction where the arrow reached furthest. After this is done the King returns home, and on that day he fasts and with him all the people of the land; and on the next day he goes to the river to bathe with all his people. Within these nine days the King is paid all the rents that he receives from his kingdom; for, as already said, all the land belongs to the King, and from his hand the captains hold it. They make it over to the husbandmen who pay nine-tenths to their lord; and they have no land of their own, for the kingdom belongs entirely to the King;[2] only the captains are put to charges on account of the troops for whom the King makes them responsible, and whom they are obliged to provide in the way of service. Every Saturday the dancing-girls are obliged to go to the palace to dance and posture before the King's idol, which is in the interior of his palace. The people of this country always fast on Saturdays and do not eat all day nor even at night, nor do they drink water, only they may chew a few cloves to sweeten the breath. The King always gives large sums in charity; in the palace there are always two or three thousand Brahmans who are his priests, and to whom the King commands to give alms. These Brahman priests are very despicable men; they always have much money, and are so insolent that even by

[1] The Qutb Shâh of Golkonda.

[2] Whether true or not, this statement, coming as it does from a totally external source, strongly supports the view often held that the ryots of South India were grievously oppressed by the nobles when subject to Hindu government. Other passages in both these chronicles, each of which was written quite independently of the other, confirm the assertion here made as to the mass of the people being ground down and living in the greatest poverty and distress.

using blows the guards of the door cannot hold them in check.

The captains and principal people use[1] at night torches of oil, from four to twelve torches (according to rank), those of highest rank having twelve at most. The King, however, must have a hundred or a hundred and fifty torches. There is much wax in the country, but they do not know how to work it. Every merchant who brings merchandise in horses and other things which he may have brought to sell to the King, if he desires an audience, has to offer him a present of a piece of goods or a horse of the best that he has brought, in order that he may obtain an audience and transact his business. And this not only to the King. You must perforce pay bribes to all the several officers with whom you have to deal. They will do nothing without some profit to themselves.

When any one suffers wrong and wishes to represent his case to the King he shows how great is his suffering by lying flat on his face on the ground till they ask him what it is he wants. If, perchance, he wishes to speak to the King while he is riding, he takes the shaft of a spear and ties a branch to it and thus goes along calling out. Then they make room for him, and he makes his complaint to the King; and it is there and then settled without more ado, and the King orders a captain, one of those who go with him, to do at once what the supplicant asks. If he complains that he was robbed in such and such a province and in such and such a road, the King sends immediately for the captain of that province, even though he be at court, and the captain may be seized and his property taken if he does not catch the thief. In the same way the chief bailiff[2] is obliged to give an account of the robberies in the

[1] When passing through the city, probably.
[2] *Meyrinho.*

capital, and in consequence very few thefts take place; and even if some are committed, you give some little present and a description of the man who stole from you, and they will soon know by the agency of the wizards whether the thief be in the city or not; for there are very powerful wizards in this country. Thus there are very few thieves in the land.

This King has continually fifty thousand paid soldiers, amongst whom are six thousand horsemen who belong to the palace guard, to which six thousand belong the two hundred who are obliged to ride with him. He has also twenty thousand spearmen and shield-bearers, and three thousand men to look after the elephants in the stables; he has sixteen hundred grooms[1] who attend to the horses, and has also three hundred horse trainers[2] and two thousand artificers, namely blacksmiths, masons, and carpenters, and washermen who wash clothes. These are the people he has and pays every day; he gives them their allowance at the gate of the palace. To the six thousand horsemen the King gives horses free and gives provision for them every month, and all these horses are marked with the King's mark; when they die they are obliged to take the piece of skin containing the mark to Madanarque, the chief master of the horse, so that he may give them another, and these horses which he gives are mostly country-breds which the King buys, twelve or fifteen for a thousand *pardaos*.[3] The King every year buys thirteen thousand horses of Ormuz, and country-breds, of which he chooses the best for his own stables, and he gives the rest to his captains, and gains much money by them; because after taking out the good Persian horses, he sells those which are country-bred, and gives five for a thousand *pardaos*, and they are obliged to pay him the money for them within

[1] *Farazes.*

[2] *Saneis que ensynão os cavallos.*

[3] Above, p. 361, and note.

the month of September; and with the money so obtained he pays for the Arabs that he buys of the Portuguese, in such a way that his captains pay the cost of the whole without anything going out of the Treasury.

This King has also within his gates more than four thousand women, all of whom live in the palace; some are dancing-girls, and others are bearers[1] who carry the King's wives on their shoulders, and the King also in the interior of the palace, for the king's houses are large and there are great intervals between one house and another. He has also women who wrestle, and others who are astrologers and soothsayers; and he has women who write all the accounts of expenses that are incurred inside the gates, and others whose duty it is to write all the affairs of the kingdom and compare their books with those of the writers outside; he has women also for music, who play instruments and sing. Even the wives of the King are well versed in music.

The King has other women besides. He has ten cooks for his personal service, and has others kept for times when he gives banquets; and these ten prepare the food for no one save for the King alone. He has a eunuch for guard at the gate of the kitchen, who never allows any one to enter for fear of poison. When the King wishes to eat, every person withdraws, and then come some of the women whose duty it is and they prepare the table for him; they place for him a three-footed stool, round, made of gold, and on it put the messes. These are brought in large vessels of gold, and the smaller messes in basins of gold, some of which are adorned with precious stones. There is no cloth on the table, but one is brought when the King has finished

[1] *Bois*. Hindu women of the Boyi caste. The Boyis are Telugus, and are employed as bearers of palanqueens and other domestic service in Southern India. Hence the Anglo-Indian term "Boy" for a servant.

eating, and he washes his hands and mouth. Women and eunuchs serve him at table. The wives of the King remain each in her own chamber and are waited on by maid-servants. It is said that he has judges, as well as bailiffs and watchmen who every night guard the palace, and all these are women.

The King never puts on any garment more than once, and when he takes it off he at once delivers it to certain officers who have charge of this duty, and they render an account; and these garments are never given to any one. This is considered to show great state. His clothes are silk cloths (*pachõiis*)[1] of very fine material and worked with gold, which are worth each one ten *pardaos;* and they wear at times *bajuris* of the same sort, which are like shirts with a skirt; and on the head they wear caps of brocade which they call *culaes*,[2] and one of these is worth some twenty cruzados. When he lifts it from his head he never again puts it on.

The punishments that they inflict in this kingdom are these: for a thief, whatever theft he commits, howsoever little it be, they forthwith cut off a foot and a hand, and if his theft be a great one he is hanged with a hook under his chin. If a man outrages a respectable woman or a virgin he has the same punishment, and if he does any other such violence his punishment is of a like kind. Nobles who become traitors are sent to be impaled alive on a wooden stake thrust through the belly, and people of the lower orders, for whatever crime they commit, he forthwith commands to cut off their heads in the market-place, and the same for a murder unless the death was the result of a duel. For great honour is done to those who fight in a duel, and they give the estate of the dead man to the survivor; but no one fights a duel without first asking leave of the minister,

[1] See above, note to p. 377.
[2] Telugu, *kuḷḷāyi*. See pp. 210, 252, 273.

who forthwith grants it. These are the common kinds of punishments, but they have others more fanciful; for when the King so desires, he commands a man to be thrown to the elephants, and they tear him in pieces. The people are so subject to him that, if you told a man on the part of the King that he must stand still in a street holding a stone on his back all day till you released him, he would do it.

The officers of the King who go about the kingdom are these:—First the minister (*regedor*) of the kingdom, who is the second person in it, then the treasurer, with the scribes of the King's own lands,[1] the chief treasurer, and the commander of the palace guards (*o porteiro moor*), the treasurer of the jewels, the chief master of the horse. The King has no controller of the revenues nor other officers, nor officers of his house, but only the captains of his kingdom; of whom I will here mention some, and the revenues they hold, and of what territory they are lords,

Firstly Salvanayque, the present minister; he has a revenue of a million and a hundred thousand gold *pardaos*. He is lord of Charamãodel and of Nagapatão, and Tamgor, and Bomgarin, and Dapatao, and Truguel, and Caullim, and all these are cities; their territories are all very large, and they border on Ceylon.[2] Of this

[1] *De fazemda.* I think that the meaning is as given. It will be observed below that the kingdom was divided into provinces or estates, each one entrusted to a noble who farmed the revenue to his own advantage, paying a fixed sum every year to the king. In the case of Narvara, the treasurer of the jewels, his estate is described as "bordering on the country of Bisnaga," and as this expression cannot refer to the entire country ruled by the king, it must be taken in a limited sense as applying to the king's own personal lands—his home-farm, so to speak. The system is well known in India, where a prince holds what are called *Khâs* lands, *i.e.* lands held privately for his own personal use and benefit, as distinct from the lands held under him by others, the revenue of which last ought to go to the public purse.

[2] Note that Madura is not mentioned in these lists. And yet it would appear that a Nâyakka, or subordinate chief of Vijayanagar, had been

money he is obliged to give a third to the King, and two-thirds remain for him for the expenses of his *lascarís* and horses, which he is obliged to maintain for the King, viz.: thirty thousand foot and three thousand horse and thirty elephants; so that he only gets the balance after deducting the expenses of this force. But in this way he acquires much wealth because he never maintains the whole force. And the King, whenever he wishes, takes away property of these nobles.

Another captain, Ajaparcatimapa,[1] who was minister of Crisnarao, has a revenue of eight hundred thousand *pardaos* of gold, and is lord of the city of Hudogary,[2] and of the city of Condovim,[3] and of the city of

ruling at that place since 1499. Mr. Nelson, in his work, "The Madura Country," gives the following list of Nayâkkas there :—

	A.D.
Narasa Nâyakka	1499–1500
Tenna Nâyakka	1500–1515
Narasa Pillai (a Tamulian)	1515–1519
Kuru Kuru Timmappa Nâyakka	1519–1524
Kattiyama Kâmayya Nâyakka	1524–1526
Chinnappa Nâyakka	1526–1530
Ayyakârai Veyyappa Nâyakka	1530–1535
Visvanâtha Nâyakka Ayyar	1535–1544

Four others are mentioned before we come to the great Visvanâtha Nâyakka, who founded an hereditary dynasty, though himself only a deputy of the crown. He ruled Madura from 1559 to 1563. Muttu Krishnappa (1602–1609) seems to have been the first to assume royal titles at Madura. His son, Muttu Vîrappa (1609–1623), is stated, in the narrative of the Portuguese writer Barradas (above, p. 230), to have paid a tribute in A.D. 1616 to the Vijayanagar king at Chandragiri of 600,000 pagodas; he had several vassal kings under him, and must have already obtained great power. It is possible that, in the time of Nuniz, Madura was not one of the greater provinces, but that it became so later.

The names Choromandel, Negapatam, and Tanjore are easy to distinguish in this list. "Bomgarin" I cannot identify, though the termination, *garim*, may represent *giri*, "mountain." "Dapatao" may be Devipatnam. "Truguel" seems to have some affinity with Tirukovil. It cannot be the "Truguel" mentioned by Barros and others as one of the fortresses given to Asada Khân by the king of Vijayanagar (above, p. 175), because those were close to Belgaum, while this "Truguel" was in the extreme south. "Caullim" may be Kayal.

[1] Above, p. 360, note 1. [2] Udayagiri. [3] Kondavíd.

2 B

Penagundim,[1] and of Codegaral[2] of Cidaota.[3] All these large cities border on the kingdom of Oria, and some of them with Cape Comorin (*cabo de Comarỹ*). These lands Crisnarao gave him when he made him minister and put out the eyes of Salvatinica, his minister, who was captain of them. He is obliged to serve with twenty-five thousand[4] foot, fifteen hundred horse, and forty elephants, and pays each year to the King three hundred thousand *pardaos.*

Another captain, who is called Gapanayque, is lord of these lands, namely of Rosyl,[5] and of Tipar, and of Ticalo, and of Bigolom.[6] These lands march with the territory of the Ydallcão, and in all these there is much wheat and grains and cattle and goats and gingely and cotton; and very fine cloth made of the last, for all the cloth that is manufactured is made of it. He has a revenue from these territories of six hundred thousand *pardaos,* and is obliged to furnish two thousand five hundred horse, and twenty thousand foot, and twenty elephants, and he pays every year to the King a hundred and fifty thousand *pardaos.*

Another captain called Lepapayque, who is lord of Vimgapor,[7] a land very rich in seed-plots and cattle-breeding farms, has a revenue of three hundred thousand *pardaos;* and is obliged to furnish twelve hundred horse and twenty thousand foot and twenty-eight elephants,

[1] Pennakonda. [2] (?) Kanigiri, Nellore district.

[3] Siddhout or Siddhavattam, Cuddapah district. Codegaral *may* represent Gandikota, the termination *giri*, "hill," being substituted for *kota*, "fort," *e.g. Gandigiri.*

[4] The passage is incomplete, and I have rendered it as seems reasonable. It runs, "*vinte e cimco mill e quinhentos de cavallo e*," &c. Looking at the other lists of troops, it cannot be supposed that this chief had to provide 25,000 horse. It seems more probable that such a word as *piães* was accidentally omitted after *mill*, and that *mill* should have been repeated before *quinhentos.*

[5] Perhaps Rachol, near Goa.

[6] Bicholim (?).

[7] "Bengapor" as elsewhere spelt, *i.e.* Bankâpur, south of Dhârwâr.

and he pays to the King every year eighty thousand *pardaos*.

The treasurer of the jewels, who is called Narvara, is captain of the new city which is called Ondegema,[1] and is lord of the city of Diguoty and of Darguem and of Entarem,[2] and of the other lands bordering on the lands of Bisnaga; they are all fields. They yield him every year four hundred thousand *pardaos*, of which he gives the King two hundred thousand, and the rest he spends on twelve thousand foot and six hundred horse and twenty elephants.

Another captain called Chinapanayque, the King's marshal, is lord of the land of Calalỹ[3] in the direction of Cochim in the interior, and of many other lands that yield him three hundred thousand *pardaos*; and he is obliged to pay the King every year one hundred thousand *pardaos*, and serves with eight hundred horse and ten thousand foot (*praços*).

Crisnapanayque is lord of Aõsel,[4] which is a large

[1] See the last sentence of the chronicle of Paes (above, p. 290), where a town "on the east" is called the new city which Krishna Deva built in honour of his favourite wife. The writer has evidently been confused in that statement, for it seems clear that the town so founded was Nâgalâpur, the old name for Hospett, with which it is distinctly identified in other places. This town "on the east" is said, in the sentence referred to, to bear the name "Ardegema," and the locality is hard to determine. "East" of what? If east of Nâgalâpur be meant, then Ardegema or Ondegema (*gema* probably represents *grâma*, "village") might have been a suburb of that town. If east of the capital be intended, I cannot identify the place. But these places evidently were close to the capital, bordering on the crown lands. This, I take it, is the meaning of "bordering on the lands (*terra*) of Bisnaga."

[2] These three places I cannot identify. "Diguoty" may perhaps be Duggavatti, in the Harpanhalli division of the Bellary district. "Darguem" suggests "Droog" or "Durgam." The word is applied to a hill-fort, of which there are many in the neighbourhood. One of the most important was Râyadrûg, south of Bellary. One of the ghât roads leading eastwards from Goa is called the "gate de Digui" in old maps.

[3] Possibly Kalale in Mysore, a place fifteen miles south of that capital. It is said to have been founded in 1504 by a noble who was connected with the Vijayanagar royal family (Rice's Gazetteer, ii. 255).

[4] Unidentified

city, and of other villages that I do not here mention as they have very difficult names. These lands yield him every year twenty thousand *pardaos* of gold, and he pays an annual revenue to the King of seven thousand *pardaos*, and serves with five hundred horse and seven hundred foot (*praços*).

Also Bajapanarque, who is captain of the country of Bodial,[1] which borders on Mamgalor[2] by the sea-coast. He is lord too of Guiana.[3] In this country there is much pepper and sugar-cane and cloth (of flax)[4] and much rice; but there is no wheat, nor other cloth, and it is a land of wax. It yields him three hundred thousand *pardaos* a year, and he serves with eight hundred horsemen and ten thousand foot and fifteen elephants. He pays the King ten thousand *pardaos*.

Mallpanarque, who was chief master of the horse to King Crisnarao, is lord of the country of Avaly,[5] which is in the interior of Calecu.[6] This land has much iron and much cotton, rice, goats, sheep, cows and buffaloes. He has a revenue of fifteen thousand *pardaos*, and is obliged to serve with four hundred horse and six thousand foot, and pays the King every year five thousand *pardaos*.

Another captain, called Adapanayque, who is the chief counsellor of the King, is lord of the country of Gate,[7] whence come the diamonds, and of many other

[1] Perhaps Budehâl in Mysore, which like Kalale was founded by a Vijayanagar officer, and contains several sixteenth-century inscriptions. It is in the Chittaldrûg division, forty miles south of that place.

[2] Mangalore.

[3] Unidentified.

[4] *Roupa*. Linen cloth. The word is not used of cotton, and the next sentence shows that cotton did not grow in that tract.

[5] I hazard the suggestion that this may be a mistake of the copyist for "Avâti." This place, now a village in the Kolar district of Mysore, was in the fifteenth century an important place, a ruling family having been founded here by the "Morasu Wokkalu" or "Seven Farmers" (Rice, "Mysore and Coorg," ii. 20). The description applies to it fairly well.

[6] Calicut.

[7] Either "the ghâts," or perhaps Gutti (Gooty). The rich Vajra Karûr diamond mines are about twenty miles south-west of Gooty, where are the remains of a very fine hill-fortress.

territories which yield him three hundred thousand gold *pardaos*, excluding the precious stones which form a revenue by themselves. He pays to the King every year forty thousand *pardaos*, with the condition that all diamonds which exceed twenty *mangelins*[1] in weight shall be given to the King for his Treasury. He serves with eight thousand foot and eight hundred horse and thirty elephants, and pays the King every year one hundred thousand *pardaos*.

Another Bajapanayque is captain of Mumdoguel,[2] which was a fortress of the Ydalcão, and was taken from him by Crisnarao when he took Rachol,[3] which was a boundary of it. This fortress of Mumdoguel with other territories yields him four hundred thousand *pardaos*, and he serves with a thousand cavalry and ten thousand foot and fifty elephants, and pays the King every year one hundred and fifty thousand *pardaos*.

In this way the kingdom of Bisnaga is divided between more than two hundred captains who are all heathen,[4] and according to the lands and revenues that they have so the King settles for them the forces that they are compelled to keep up, and how much revenue they have to pay him every month during the first nine days of the month of September. He never gives any receipts to them, only, if they do not pay they are well punished, and are ruined and their property taken away. All the captains of this kingdom make use of litters and palanqueens. These are like biers and men carry them on their shoulders, but people are not allowed to make use of litters unless they are cavaliers of the highest rank, and the captains and principal persons use palanqueens. There are always at the court where the King is twenty thousand litters and palanqueens.

[1] See note above, p. 368. [2] Mudkal. [3] Raichûr.
[4] *I.e.* of the Hindu religion, not Muhammadans.

These matters concerning (*i.e.* the power and greatness of) the kingdom of Bisnaga, though it may seem to you that I have exaggerated, yet the people of this country assert them to have been even more notable[1] in times past, and greater than they now are.

And in this kingdom of Bisnaga there is a class of men, natives of the country, namely Brahmans, who the most part of them never kill or eat any live thing, and these are the best that there are amongst them. They are honest men, given to merchandise, very acute and of much talent, very good at accounts, lean men and well-formed, but little fit for hard work. By these and by the duties they undertake the kingdom is carried on. They believe that there are Three Persons and only One God, and they call the Persons of the Most Holy Trinity "*Tricebemca*." There is another class who are Canarese who have pagodas in which are (images of?) monkeys, and cows, and buffaloes, and devils, to whom they pay much honour, and these idols and monkeys which they adore they say that in former times this land belonged all to the monkeys, and that in those days they could speak. They have books full of fine stories of chivalry, and many foolish tales about their idols, such as it is out of reason for men to believe. But because of this, neither in the kingdom of Bisnaga nor in all the land of the heathen are any monkeys killed, and there are so many in this country that they cover the mountains. There is another class of men called Telumgalle;[2] when these die their wives are buried alive with them.

The King of Bisnaga is a Brahman;[3] every day he hears the preaching of a learned Brahman, who never married nor ever touched a woman. He urges in his preaching (obedience to) the commandments of God, that is to say, that one must not kill any living thing, nor take

[1] *Noveis* in the original, probably for *notaveis*.

[2] Telugus.

[3] This was certainly not the case.

anything belonging to another, and as with these so with the rest of the commandments. These people have such devotion to cows that they kiss them every day, some they say even on the rump—a thing I do not assert for their honour—and with the droppings of these cows they absolve themselves from their sins as if with holy water. They have for a commandment to confess their sins to the Brahman priests, but they do not do it, except only those who are very religious (*amiguos de Dios*). They give in excuse that they feel a shame to confess themselves to another man, and say that it is sufficient to confess themselves alone after approaching God, for he who does not do so does not acquire grace; thus they fulfil the command in one way or another. But they do it so seldom (in reality) that they (may be said to) neglect this command to confess.

This kingdom of Bisnaga is all heathen. The women have the custom of burning themselves when their husbands die, and hold it an honour to do so. When therefore their husbands die they mourn with their relations and those of their husbands, but they hold that the wife who weeps beyond measure has no desire to go in search of her husband; and the mourning finished their relations speak to them, advising them to burn themselves and not to dishonour their generation. After that, it is said, they place the dead man on a bed with a canopy of branches and covered with flowers, and they put the woman on the back of a worthless horse, and she goes after them with many jewels on her, and covered with roses; she carries a mirror in her hand and in the other a branch of flowers, and (she goes accompanied by) many kinds of music, and his relations (go with her) with much pleasure. A man goes also playing on a small drum, and he sings songs to her telling her that she is going to join her husband, and she answers also in singing that so she will do. As soon as she arrives at the place where they are always burned she waits with the musicians till her husband is burned, whose body they place in a very large pit that has been made ready for it, covered with much firewood. Before they light the fire his mother or his nearest relative takes a vessel of water on the head and a firebrand in the hand, and goes three times round the pit, and at each round makes a hole in the pot; and when these three rounds are done breaks the pot, which is small, and throws the torch into the pit. Then they apply the fire, and when the body is burned comes the wife with all the feasters and washes her feet, and then a Brahman performs over her certain ceremonies according to their law; and when he has finished doing this, she draws off with her own hand all the jewels that she wears, and divides them among her female relatives, and if she has sons she commends them to her most honoured relatives. When they have taken off all she has on, even her good clothes, they put on her some common yellow cloths, and her relatives take her hand and she takes a branch in the other, and goes singing and running to the pit where the fire is, and then mounts on some steps which are made high up by the pit. Before they do this they go three times round the fire, and then she mounts the steps and holds in front of her a mat that prevents her from seeing the fire. They throw into the fire a cloth containing rice, and another in which they carry betel leaves, and her comb and mirror with which she adorned herself, saying that all these are needed to adorn herself by her husband's side. Finally she takes leave of all, and puts a pot of oil on her head, and casts herself into the fire with such courage that it is a thing of wonder; and as soon as she throws herself in, the relatives are ready with firewood and quickly cover her with it, and after this is done they all raise loud lamentations. When a captain dies, however many wives he has thev all burn themselves, and when the King dies they do the same. This is the custom throughout all the country of the heathen, except with that caste of people called Telugas, amongst whom the wives are buried alive with their husbands when they die. These go with much pleasure to the pit, inside of which are made two seats of earth, one for him and one for her, and they place each one on his own seat and cover them in little by little till they are covered up; and so the wife dies with the husband.

CHAPTER XXIII

Of the ceremonies practised at the death of Brahmans.

When a Brahman is sick, before he dies, they send to call the learned Brahmans who are his priests, so that they should come to pray, and console the sick man; and they talk to him of the affairs of his soul, and what he must do to save it, bidding him spend money in alms. After this ceremony is over they make the Brahman priests shave the sick man's head, and after the shaving they bid them wash it, and after the washing it is their custom to bring into their houses a cow with a calf,—there are very few Brahmans, however poor they be, who do not have one to live in their house,—which cow, when they have finished washing the man's head, they take a turban and tie it to its neck and put the end of the turban into the hand of the sick man, and he gives it and the calf in alms for his soul to those priests who perform these ceremonies. On that day he gives alms according to his position, and gives to eat to some Brahmans who are invited and who come there for the purpose. They believe that when these ceremonies are made for the sick man, if he is to live he is soon cured of his infirmity, and if not that he soon dies.

After the death of the sick man they have the ground washed upon which he lay, and after the washing they take cow-dung and spread it over the ground, and place the body on the top of this dung. They hold that a sick man who dies on a cot, or on anything soever except only on the ground, commits a mortal sin. As soon as the body is laid on the ground they make for it a bier covered with boughs of the fig-tree, and before they place the body on the bier they wash it well with pure water, and anoint it with sandal-wood (oil); and they place by the body branches of sweet basil and cover it with a new cloth, and so place it in the bier. Then one of his relatives takes the bier on one side, and they call three other Brahmans whosoever they may be to aid them to lift it; and so they carry it to the place where they are to burn it, accompanied by many Brahmans who go singing in front of the corpse. In front of all goes his son, if he has one, or next younger brother or nearest relative, with fire in the hand for the burning. As soon as they arrive at the place where they have to burn the body, they scatter money according to their ability, and then put the fire to it; and they wait there till the whole body is consumed, and then all go and wash their bodies in a tank and afterwards return each one to his house. The son or brother or relation who put the fire is obliged to sleep on the ground where the man died for nine nights, and after the lapse of nine days from the death come the priests and learned men and they command to shave the head of this man. During these nine days, they feed the poor and they give them the dead man's clothes, and they give the cot with its bed in alms to the priests, with some money in addition; if he is a rich man they give gardens and other things in alms to many Brahmans. When ten days are finished, and the son has been shaved, he goes to the place where they burned his father or his brother, and they perform many ceremonies over the ashes and bones that remain unburned; then they put them in a small vessel and make a pit in the ground and bury them in it, and keep them thus guarded and buried in order (afterwards) to send the bones to be thrown into a sacred river, which is distant from Goa over one thousand leagues.[1] There is a very large temple there, the object of many pilgrimages, and they hold that every pilgrim who dies there is saved, and goes to Paradise, and also every dead man whose bones are thrown into that river. In spite of this they in reality take very few people there. The heir or the father or son of the dead man is obliged,, from the day of the death, for eleven days to give food to twenty-seven Brahmans, and until twenty-one days to three others; until twelve days again he feeds seven Brahmans, and until twenty-seven days gives to eat to the three; on the last day of the month he gives food to three others, and thenceforward, until one year is finished, he gives meals once a month to three Brahmans. They do this in honour of the Trinity for the soul of the deceased. When this year is over he gives no more alms, except that each year, on the day on which the death happened, he feeds six Brahmans,—namely, three in honour of the Trinity, and three for the persons of his father, grandfather, and great-grandfather; who thus seemingly eat together. Thus he obtains favour with God, and for these expenses they beg alms of the Brahmans if they are poor. These give him all help for it. Before they dine they wash the feet of all six, and during the meal some ceremonies are performed by Brahman priests who come there for that purpose.

[1] The Ganges.

APPENDICES

APPENDIX A

DIAMONDS

HOWEVER much it may at first sight appear that our chroniclers have exaggerated in their description of the wealth of the Hindu sovereign and his nobles, and of the wonderful display of jewels made on days of high festival by the ladies of their households, an account of which is given us by Paes, I for one see little reason for doubt. Nuniz distinctly states (p. 389) that the diamond mines, in their day the richest in the world, were farmed out on condition that all stones above twenty mangellins in weight— about twenty-five carats—were sent to the Râya for his personal use, and there must have been many of these. Barradas (p. 226 above) states that, according to rumour, even after the downfall of the empire the king at Chandragiri in 1614 A.D. had no less than three large chests full of diamonds in his possession; and every traveller and chronicler has something to say on the subject.

The principal mines were on the north bank of the Krishnâ river, and in the Kurnool and Anantapur countries, notably at Vajra Karûr. Generically these are known as "the mines of Golkonda," and the phrase has passed into a proverb.

Linschoten (ii. 136) writes: "They (diamonds) grow in the countrie of Decam behinde Ballagate, by the towne of Bisnagar, wherein are two or three hilles, from whence they are digged, whereof the King of Bisnagar doth reape great profitte; for he causeth them to be straightly watched, and hath farmed them out with this condition, that all diamonds that are above twenty-five Mangellyns in waight are for the King himselfe (every Mangellyn is foure graines in waight).

"There is yet another hill in the Countrie of Decam, which is called Velha, that is the old Rocke, from whence come the best diamonds and are sold for the greatest price. . . . Sometimes they find Diamonds of one hundred and two hundred Mangelyns and more, but very few."

As regards the diamond "as large as a hen's egg," said to have been found at the sack of Vijayanagar and presented to the Âdil Shâh (above, p. 208), Couto (Decada VIII. c. xv.) says that it was a jewel which the Râya had affixed to the base of the plume on his horse's head-dress. Garcia da Orta, who was in India in 1534, says that at Vijayanagar a diamond had been seen as large as a small hen's egg, and he even declares the weights of three others to have been respectively 120, 148, and 250 *mangelis*, equivalent to 150, 175, and 312½ carats (Tavernier, V. Ball, ii. 433).

Dr. Ball has gone carefully into the question of the diamonds known as "Bâbar's," "the Mogul's," "Pitt's," "the *Koh-i-nûr*," and others, and to his Appendix I. I beg to refer those interested in the subject.

It is clear that this hen's egg diamond could not be the same as Sultan Bâbar's, because the former was taken at Vijayanagar in A.D. 1565, whereas Sultan Bâbar's was received by his son Humâyun at Agra in 1526, and could not have been, forty years later, in the possession of the Hindu king of the south.[1]

Dr. Ball has shown that probably the *Koh-i-nûr* is identical with the "Mogul's diamond." Was, then, this "hen's egg" diamond the same? Probably not. If we had been told that the "hen's egg," when found in the sack of Vijayanagar, had been cut, the proof *contra* would be conclusive, since the *Koh-i-nûr* was certainly uncut in A.D. 1656 or 1657. But there is no information available on this point.

The "hen's egg" was apparently taken by the Âdil Shâh to Bîjapûr in 1565, and it is not likely to have found its way, still in an uncut state, into the possession of Mîr Jumla in 1656.

The *Koh-i-nûr* was found at Kollûr on the river Krishnâ, probably in A.D. 1656. Mîr Jumla farmed the mines at that time, and presented it uncut to the emperor, Shâh Jahân. It is said to have weighed 756 English carats (Ball, ii. 444). It was entrusted to a Venetian named Hortensio Borgio, and was so damaged and wasted in his hands that, when seen by Tavernier in Aurangzîb's treasury in 1665, it weighed not more than 268½ English carats. In 1739 Nadir Shâh sacked Delhi and carried the stone away with him to Persia, conferring on it its present immortal name the "Mountain of Light." On his murder in 1747 it passed into the hands of his grandson, Shâh Rukh. Four years later Shâh Rukh gave it to Ahmad Shâh Durâni of Kâbul, and by him it

[1] Its history is known from A.D. 1304, when it was acquired by Alâ-ud-Dîn Khilji from the Rajah of Malwa.

was bequeathed to his son Taimûr. In 1793 it passed by descent to his son Shâh Zamân, who was blinded and deposed by his brother Muhammad; but he retained possession of the stone in his prison, and in 1795 it became the property of his brother Sultan Shuja. In 1809, after Shuja became king of Kabul, Elphinstone saw the diamond in his bracelet at Peshawur. In 1812, Shuja, being dethroned by Muhammad, fled to Lahore, where he was detained as a quasi-prisoner by Ranjît Singh, the ruler of the Panjâb. In 1813 an agreement was arrived at, and Shuja surrendered the diamond to Ranjît Singh. Ranjît often wore the stone, and it was constantly seen by European visitors to Lahore. Dying in 1839, the *Koh-i-nûr* was placed in the jewel-chamber till the infant Dhulîp Singh was acknowledged as Ranjît's successor. In 1849 it was handed over to Sir John Lawrence on the annexation of the Panjâb, and by him was sent to England to Her Majesty the Queen. In 1851 it was exhibited at the first great Exhibition, and in 1852 it was re-cut by an Amsterdam cutter, Voorsânger, in the employ of Messrs. Garrards. The weight is now $106\frac{1}{16}$ carats.

It would be interesting to trace the story of the "hen's egg" diamond after its acquisition by the Bîjapûr sultan, Ali Âdil.

H. de Montfart, who travelled in India in 1608, saw a very large diamond in the possession of the Mogul emperor Jahângîr at Delhi,[1] but this had been pierced. "I have seene one with the great *Mogor* as bigge as a Hen's egge, and of that very forme, which he caused expressly to bee pierced like a pearle to weare it on his arme. . . . It weighteth 198 Mangelins."

[1] De Montfart's "Survey of all the East Indies." Translation, edition of 1615, p. 34.

APPENDIX B

THE WEALTH OF THE DAKHAN IN THE FOURTEENTH CENTURY A.D.

WHEN Malik Kâfur, in the year 1310 A.D., during the reign of Alâ-ud-Dîn Khilji of Delhi, carried out his successful raids into the Dakhan and to the Malabar coast, sacking all the Hindu temples, ravaging the territory of Maisûr, and despoiling the country, he is said to have returned to Delhi with an amount of treasure that seems almost fabulous. Firishtah writes: "They found in the temples prodigious spoils, such as idols of gold adorned with precious stones, and other rich effects consecrated to Hindu worship;" and Malik presented his sovereign with "312 elephants, 20,000 horses, 96,000 *mâns* of gold, several boxes of jewels and pearls, and other precious effects."

When we come to estimate the amount of gold we are met with a difficulty, as there are many varieties of *mâns* in India, the variation being as much as from 19 lbs. in Travancore to 163¼ lbs. in Ahmadnagar. The Madras *mân* weighs 25 lbs., the Bombay *mân* 28 lbs. Hawkins, writing in 1610, gives 55 lbs. to the *mân*,[1] Middleton, in 1611, 33 lbs.[2] Now Firishtah had more to do with Ahmadnagar than any other part of India, and if his estimate was based on the *mân* of that tract, Malik Kâfur's 96,000 *mâns* of gold would have amounted to the enormous sum of 15,672,000 lbs. weight. It is hardly likely that Firishtah would have had in his mind the Travancore *mân*. Even if he was thinking of the Madras *mân*, which is not likely, his estimate of the weight of the gold carried off amounted to 2,400,000 lbs.

Whether we accept these amounts or not, there can be no manner of doubt that the richness of the temples was very great, and the reason is easy to see. The country had always been subject to Hindu kings, and treasures had year by year accumulated. The Brahmans exacted gifts and payments from the people

[1] Purchas, i. 218.

[2] See Yule and Burnell's Dictionary, *s.v.* "Maund."

on all occasions. Kings and chiefs, merchants and landowners, vied with one another in presenting rich offerings to their favourite places of worship; and when it is remembered that this practice had been going on from time immemorial, it need be no matter for wonder that the man who first violently despoiled the sacred buildings departed from the country laden with an almost incredible amount of booty. Colonel Dow, in his translation of the works of Firishtah (i. 307), computes the value of the gold carried off by Malik Kâfur at a hundred millions sterling of our money.

APPENDIX C

TABLES FOR REFERENCE

APPROXIMATE DATES OF REIGNS OF KINGS OF VIJAYANAGAR

The First Dynasty.

King	A.D.
HARIHARA I.	1336 to 1343
BUKKA I.	1343 to 1379

(*Certain inscriptions imply that Kampa reigned from* 1343 *to* 1355, *and that his son Sangama was reigning in May* 1356.)

King	A.D.
HARIHARA II.	1379 to end of 1399
BUKKA II.	end of 1399 to Nov. 1406
DEVA RÂYA I.	Nov. 1406 to 1412–13
VÎRA VIJAYA	1412–13 to 1419
DEVA RÂYA II.	1419 to 1444 (?)
——— (?)	(?) 1444 to 1449
MALLIKÂRJUNA	1452–53, 1464–65
RÂJASÊKHARA	1468–69
VIRÛPÂKSHA I.	1470–71
(?) PRAUDHA DEVA RÂYA	1476–77 (?)
RÂJASÊKHARA	1479–80
VIRÛPÂKSHA II.	1483–84
RÂJASÊKHARA	1486–87

Confused period. The dates given are those of inscriptions. (Mallikârjuna to Râjasêkhara, 1452–1487)

The Second Dynasty.

King	A.D.
NARASIMHA	(?) 1490 to (?)
NARASA or VÎRA NARASIMHA	(?) to 1509
KRISHNA DEVA RÂYA	1509 to 1530
ACHYUTA	1530 to 1542
SADÂSIVA (*a prisoner all his life*)	1542 to 1567

The Third Dynasty.

King	A.D.
RÂMA (*practically sovereign*)	1542 to 1565
TIRUMALA (*practically sovereign*)	1565 to 1567
,, (*actually king*)	1567 to 1575 (?)
RANGA II.	1575 to 1586
VENKATA I.	1586 to 1614

(*For the remainder see the text, pp.* 214, 216.)

GENEALOGY OF THE BAHMANÎ DYNASTY[1]

(According to the "Burhân-i Maâsir.")

- 1. Alâ-ud-Dîn Hasan.
  - 2. Muhammad I.
    - 3. Mujâhid.
    - Fath Khân.
  - Mahmûd Khân.
    - 4. Dâûd.
    - 5. Muhammad II.
      - 6. Ghiyâs-ud-dîn.
      - 7. Shams-ud-dîn.
  - Ahmad Khân.
    - 8. Fîrûz.
      - Hasan Khân.
      - Mubârak Khân.
        - *Makhdûmah Jahân.*
    - 9. Ahmad.
      - 10. Alâ-ud-dîn II.
        - 11. Humâyûn.
          - 12. Nizâm.
          - 13. Muhammad III.
            - 14. Mahmûd.
            - *Fatimah.*
            - *A daughter.*
          - Jamshîd.
        - Hasan Khân.
        - Yahyâ Khân.
      - Mahmûd Khân.
      - Muhammad Khân.

[1] This Table is taken from Major King's History (*Ind. Ant.*, xxviii. 121).

GENEALOGY OF THE BAHMANÎ DYNASTY[1]

(*According to Firishtah.*)

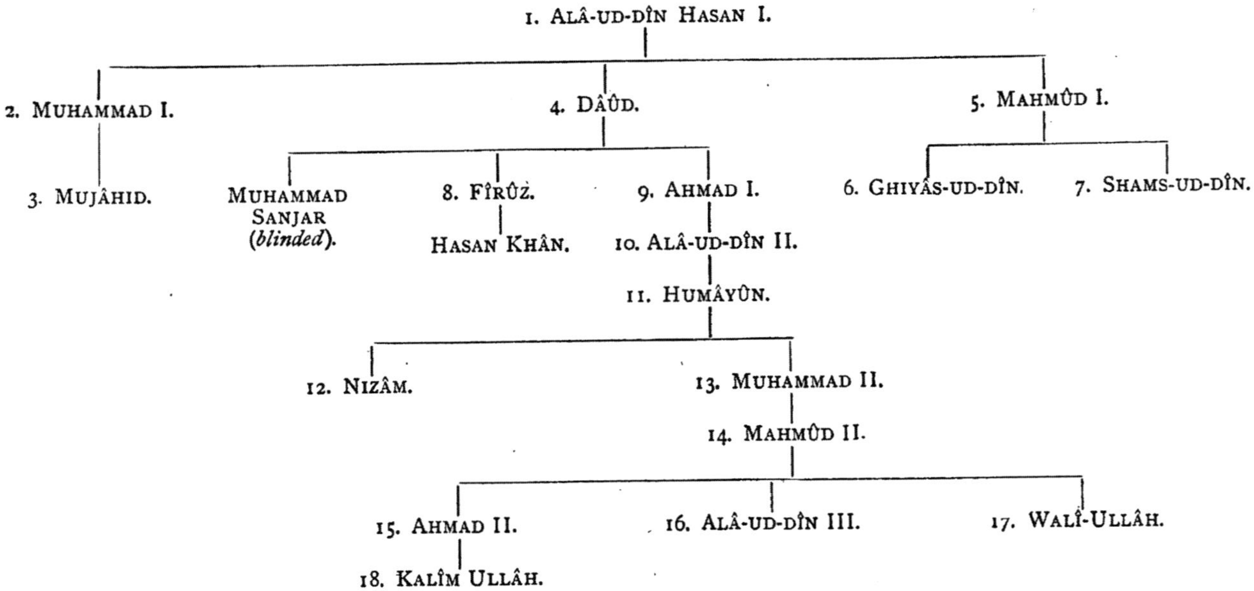

[1] This Table is taken from Major King's History (*Ind. Ant.*, xxviii. 121).

LIST OF THE BAHMANÎ SULTANS OF THE DAKHAN AT KULBARGA

(*According to Firishtah.*)

		A.D.	
1.	ALÂ-UD-DÎN BAHMANÎ I.	Aug. 3, 1347, to Feb. 2, 1358	
2.	MUHAMMAD I.	Feb. 2, 1358, to April 21, 1375	
3.	MUJÂHID	April 21, 1375, to April 16, 1378	
4.	DÂÛD	April 16 to May 21, 1378	
5.	MAHMÛD	May 21, 1378, to April 20, 1397	
6.	GHIYÂS-UD-DÎN	April 20 to June 14, 1397	
7.	SHAMS-UD-DÎN	June 14 to Nov. 15, 1397	
8.	FÎRÛZ	Nov. 15, 1397, to Sept. 24, 1422	
9.	AHMAD I.	Sept. 24, 1422, to Feb. 27, 1435	
10.	ALÂ-UD-DÎN II.	Feb. 27, 1435, to Feb. 13, 1458	
11.	HUMÂYÛN	Feb. 13, 1458, to Sept. 5, 1461	
12.	NIZÂM	Sept. 5, 1461, to July 30, 1463	
13.	MUHAMMAD	July 30, 1463, to March 21, 1482	
14.	MAHMÛD II.	March 21, 1482, to Dec. 18, 1517	
15.	AHMAD II.	Dec. 18, 1517, to (?) 1521 (?)	*Kings only in name.*
16.	ALÂ-UD-DÎN III.	1521 (?)	
17.	WALÎ-ULLÂH	(?) 1521 to (?) 1523	
18.	KALÎM ULLÂH	(?) 1523 to about 1528	

GENEALOGY OF THE ÂDIL SHÂHS OF BÎJAPÛR

- 1. ABÛ-L MUZAFFAR YUSUF ÂDIL.
  - 2. ISMÂÎL.
    - 3. MALÛ.
    - 4. IBRAHÎM.
      - 5. ALÎ.
      - TAHMASP.
        - 6. IBRAHÎM.
          - 7. MUHAMMAD.
            - 8. ALÎ.
              - 9. SIKANDAR.
        - ISMÂÎL.
    - *A daughter (m. Alâ-ud-dîn Imâd Shâh of Bîrâr).*
  - *A daughter (m. Ahmad Shâh Bâhmanî).*
  - *Maryam (m. Burhân Shâh of Ahmadnagar).*

	A.D.
1. YUSUF	1489 to 1510
2. ISMÂÎL	1510 to Aug. 27, 1534
3. MALÛ	Aug. 27, 1534, to Feb. 1535
4. IBRAHIM I.	Feb. 1535 to 1557
5. ALÎ I.	1557 to April 11, 1580
6. IBRAHÎM II.	April 11, 1580, to 1626
7. MUHAMMAD	1626 to 1656
8. ALÎ II.	1656 to 1659
9. SIKANDAR	1659 to 1686

GENEALOGY OF THE NIZÂM SHÂHS OF AHMADNAGAR

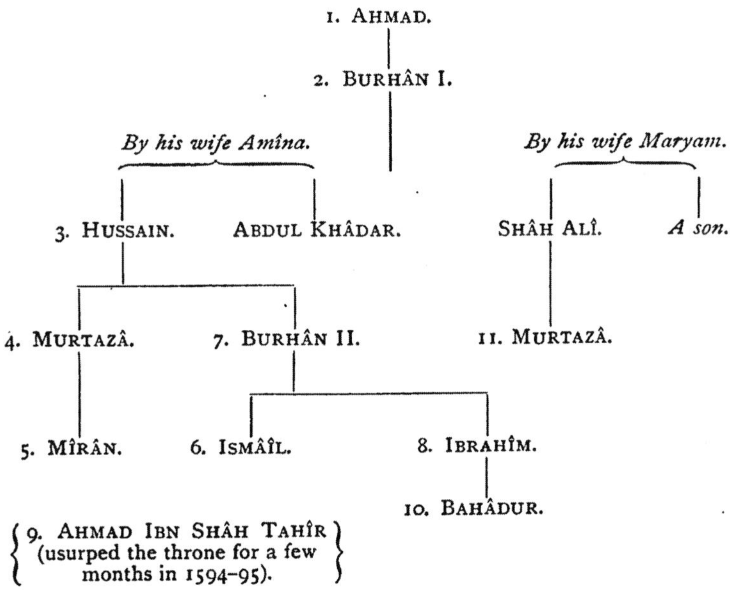

	A.D.
1. AHMAD	1490 to 1508
2. BURHÂN I.	1508 to 1553
3. HUSSAIN	1553 to 1565
4. MURTAZÂ	1565 to 1587
5. MÎRÂN	1587 to 1588
6. ISMÂÎL	1588 to 1590
7. BURHÂN II.	1590 to April 18, 1595
8. IBRAHÎM	April 18 to Aug. 6, 1595
9. AHMAD IBN SHÂH TAHÎR	Aug. 6, 1595, to 1596
10. BAHÂDUR	1596 to 1599

GENEALOGY OF THE QUTB SHÂHS OF GOLKONDA

- 1. QULÎ QUTB SHÂH.
  - QUTB-UD-DÎN (*blinded by Jamshîd*).
  - 2. JAMSHÎD.
    - SUBHÂN.
  - HAIDAR (*died without issue*).
  - 3. IBRAHÎM.
    - ABDUL QÂDIR (*poisoned by his father*).
    - *A son* (*died before his father*).
    - 4. MUHAMMAD.

	A.D.
1. QULÎ	1512 to 1543
2. JAMSHÎD	1543 to 1550
3. IBRAHÎM	1550 to 1581
4. MUHAMMAD	1581 to 1611
5. ABDULLÂH	1611 to 1672
6. ABÛ HASAN	1672 to 1688

PORTUGUESE VICEROYS AND GOVERNORS OF GOA

(A.D. 1505 *to* 1568.)

	A.D.
DOM FRANCISCO DE ALMEIDA (*Viceroy*)	1505–1509
AFONSO DE ALBUQUERQUE (*Governor*)	1509–1515
LOPO SOARES DE ALBERGARIA (*Governor*)	1515–1518
DIOGO LOPES DE SEQUEIRA (*Governor*)	1518–1521
DOM DUARTE DE MENEZES (*Governor*)	1521–1524
DOM VASCO DA GAMA, CONDE DE VIDIGUERIA (*Viceroy*) .	1524
DOM HENRIQUE DE MENEZES (*Governor*)	1525–1526
LOPO VAZ DE SAMPAIO (*Governor*)	1526–1529
NUNO DA CUNHA (*Governor*)	1529–1538
DOM GARCIA DE NORONHA (*Viceroy*)	1538–1540
DOM ESTEVÃO DA GAMA (*Governor*)	1540–1542
MARTIM AFFONSO DE SOUSA (*Governor*)	1542–1545
DOM JOÃO DE CASTRO (*Governor and Captain-in-Chief*) .	1545–1547
” ” (*Viceroy*)	1547–1548
GARCIA DE SÁ (*Governor*)	1548–1549
JORGE CABRAL (*Governor*)	1549–1550
DOM AFFONSO DE NORONHA (*Viceroy*)	1550–1554
DOM PEDRO MASCARENHAS (*Viceroy*)	1554–1555
FRANCISCO BARRETO (*Governor*)	1555–1558
DOM CONSTANTINO DE BRAGANZA (*Viceroy*)	1558–1561
DOM FRANCISCO COUTINHO, CONDE DE REDONDO (*Viceroy*)	1561–1564
JOÃO DE MEDONÇA (*Governor*)	1564
DOM ANTONIO DE NORONHA (*Viceroy*)	1564–1568

[The above List is extracted from Mr. Danvers's work, "The Portuguese in India" (vol. ii. p. 487). The author continues the List to the present day.]